This Bloody Place

This narrative of a humble share in the great adventure is dedicated with respectful admiration and esteem to

General Sir Ian Hamilton, GCB, DSO *(Colonel Gordon Highlanders)* GOC *Mediterranean Expeditionary Force*

This Bloody Place

With the Incomparable 29th

By Major A.H. Mure

Foreword by Richard van Emden

Pen & Sword
MILITARY

First published in Great Britain in 1919 by
W. & R. Chambers Ltd, London

This edition published in Great Britain in 2015 by
Pen & Sword Military
an imprint of
Pen & Sword Books Ltd
47 Church Street
Barnsley
South Yorkshire
S70 2AS

ISBN 978 1 47385 792 6

A CIP catalogue record for this book is available from the British
Library

Typeset in Ehrhardt by
Mac Style Ltd, Bridlington, East Yorkshire
Printed and bound in the UK by CPI Group (UK) Ltd, Croydon,
CRO 4YY

Pen & Sword Books Ltd incorporates the imprints of Pen & Sword
Archaeology, Atlas, Aviation, Battleground, Discovery, Family
History, History, Maritime, Military, Naval, Politics, Railways,
Select, Transport, True Crime, and Fiction, Frontline Books, Leo
Cooper, Praetorian Press, Seaforth Publishing and Wharncliffe.

For a complete list of Pen & Sword titles please contact
PEN & SWORD BOOKS LIMITED
47 Church Street, Barnsley, South Yorkshire, S70 2AS, England
E-mail: enquiries@pen-and-sword.co.uk
Website: www.pen-and-sword.co.uk

Contents

Introduction to 'With the Incomparable 29th'

One hundred years on, the Allied campaign on the Gallipoli Peninsula continues to captivate the imagination of historians and the general public alike. No other Great War operation fought beyond the boundaries of the Western Front is recalled with such interest or such horror. Gallipoli has its own particular drama, for it is hard to find another campaign that was so blindly optimistic from inception and so entirely predestined to ultimate failure, as the one that took place on Turkey's south western shores between February 1915 and January 1916.

The plan got off to the worst possible start. Founded on the Allied conceit that Turks would not stand and fight to defend their own country, it was the brainchild of the persuasive yet constitutionally restless First Lord of the Admiralty, Winston Churchill. His idea was to seek an alternative to the costly but necessary strategy of fighting and defeating Germany on the Western Front by attacking Turkey and defeating one of the Kaiser's key allies. Yet if it was thought that this would open a convenient back door to defeating Germany, then it was illusory. Knocking Turkey out of the war, it was believed, would open up a sea route to Russia's Black Sea ports, permitting the British and French to resupply their hard-pressed ally fighting on the Eastern Front. Yet the use of such a fragile supply line would hardly bring about the collapse of Germany. Churchill was fond of imaginative, broad-sweep ideas, but he was not interested in the practical detail: that was for someone else.

For the campaign to succeed, the Allies would need to press warships through 'the Narrows', a constricted, Turkish-controlled channel of water, before reaching the Sea of Marmara and sailing up to Constantinople. Unsurprisingly, this channel was guarded by Turkish forts and minefields and when an Allied naval bombardment failed to secure the safe passage of the warships, a decision was taken to land an Allied force to seize the high ground overlooking the Narrows. This landing force was ill-equipped, inexperienced and far from home; resupply would be difficult. To complete the task, it would have to sweep over nigh-impenetrable terrain, through dense shrub and across precipitous valleys, all undertaken in searing heat and under fire. It was the height of hubris and folly on the part of the men who ordered such a manoeuvre to think that this could be achieved. Some of the officers who fought contended that, with a little more support, a little more effort, success might have been assured, but this was utter nonsense. The infantry force which landed on the Gallipoli Peninsula in April 1915 never got more than spitting distance from the sea, penetrating but three miles inland at the furthest point. The soldiers were thirsty, hungry and with many suffering from dysentery were too ill to advance against a tenacious and motivated enemy. The Allied infantrymen merely clung to their insignificant gains of the spring and summer months until they were finally evacuated in January 1916.

Captain Albert Mure, commanding a company of the 5th Battalion The Royal Scots, a unit in the 29th Division, had come and long gone from Gallipoli by the time of the evacuation, indeed, the power of his story comes, in part, from the fact that his entire service was distilled into a mere 43 days. I say a mere 43 days, for this was far longer than many men who fought there would survive. In those few weeks, this brave, stoical officer was reduced from a fit, determined leader of men to a physical and mental wreck.

I have said in the past that I was once dubious as to the value of memoirs written during the Great War. All such personal recollections were meant to be forwarded to the Official Censor for approval so that books could be vetted prior to publication. Many, possibly most, books sent to the Censor were rejected for fear that they might give the enemy useful information as to the state of mind or the tactics of the British soldier. However, not all servicemen sent their memoirs to be subject to censorship. Some published their books and were prepared to take the consequences for ignoring a legal requirement. Nevertheless, I assumed that those memoirs that had passed the Censor would be superficial, rather too patriotic to be worth much attention. How wrong I was. Many of the best memoirs I have read in recent years were published during or directly after the war. There is a rawness and immediacy in much of the writing, a familiarity with events that could only dull over time. In short, a number of these books are worth their place amongst the many Great War memoirs. In this group I include Mure's 'With the Incomparable 29th', a rather dull and, on first glance, opaque title that does not reflect the superb content.

Mure is a fine writer, not least because his language is simple and above all disarmingly honest – honest about his own thoughts and emotions. He conveys the drama of the first landings as he watches the assault on the 29th Division's designated beaches, and he writes evocatively of the sense of excitement and confusion as, in the distance, he sees the small figures of the 1st Lancashire Fusiliers running over a cliff, then coming back under fire. He knows that very shortly afterwards he and his men would be ashore and into the same charnel house.

He landed and witnessed the consequences of the fight to secure the beachhead. He saw too, with evident empathy, the exhaustion on the faces of the men who survived: 'I remarked to the assistant-beachmaster, "You seem to have had a pretty thick time." He answered not a word. He only looked at me. It was enough…I turned and went away quietly, rather sheepishly.' And he captures adroitly the sense of wonderment and excitement at being on land, at war – and the sense of vulnerability too. 'I started off on a voyage of discovery along the cliff that rose abruptly behind our narrow sand-strip of beach. Before I had gone far I saw coming towards me a figure that I seemed to recognize. It turned out to be Captain Lindsay, and I was as glad to see him as if we'd been foster-brothers parted for years. It is extraordinary how your heart leaps at the sight of a familiar face at the front…'

But where Mure stands head and shoulders above so many others who wrote about their experiences is in his sympathy for his men. As company commander, he held the lives of approximately 250 men in his hands, and the responsibility always weighed heavily. Mure's remembered devotion is never mawkish or twee: he has an eye for human detail that is uncommon in Great War memoirs. So, of dealing with the possessions of the killed and wounded, he wrote:

'It was desperate work. It choked me, and I don't mind who knows it. But one thing it established in my mind for all time: "Tommy has his feelings". There were pictures of sweethearts (they said so on the back), pictures of wives, and pictures of kiddies, dressed in their best. But what touched me most, and gave me a nobler view of Tommy, were the pictures of Mother. But the saddest find of all was a pocket in which there was – nothing! Had he lived quite alone? Had no one cared? Had he not even a memory to treasure in some poor tangible token? Had he been all his life as he died – quite, quite alone?'

The 'constant crisis at Gallipoli' as Mure called it, placed immeasurable pressure on all the men, but particularly on the officers whose daily, hourly, decisions were life-changing for many. As fellow officers fell, one by one, Mure was faced with the prospect of being in command of the entire battalion, and when the acting Commanding Officer, Captain McLagan, was wounded, his turn came. McLagan was hit in the leg by a sniper. As he was carried down, Mure spoke to him briefly. Months later they were to meet again in Edinburgh. McLagan revealed what Mure had said in the trenches, though Mure had no recollection of it. 'I had said…"Damn you!" – only that, in an angry tone – and had passed on indignantly. And probably it was true. I don't think I had felt sympathetic in the least. He could ill be spared.' The responsibility for the battalion temporarily passed to Mure and he 'loathed it'.

Physically and emotionally, he was on a downward spiral. He would take part in two battles, first the fight in and around Fir Tree Wood, and secondly the ill-fated struggle for Krithia, an insignificant village. The fight for Krithia would take three battles, thousands of casualties, and would end without success. The village remained elusively out of Allied hands for the rest of the campaign. It was of negligible strategic value but was symptomatic of how the unreachable broader objectives became 'forgotten' as senior officers became obsessed by smaller and closer objectives which appeared achievable. As for Mure, the battle took away his remaining resolve; he was undoubtedly shell-shocked. What is surprising is the extent to which he would later recount his collapse. At the time he was mentally incapacitated and yet later he is able to recall his emotional breakdown in detail, unashamed and honest – to my knowledge, a rare instance of such candour. There are hours between his departure from the trenches and his appearance at the beach that he forgot; there are instances that even he saw fit to omit from his memoirs, but even so, he still tells us much that is important historically and psychologically.

'I groped around forlornly. I was dazed…I remember laughing once or twice when I heard the guns go, pleased as a child. And why not? I was a child again, a stray child, alone on Gallipoli.'

When Mure left the Peninsula by boat the following day, he was exultant and yet his 'heart clove to the battalion – the tattered battered remnants of it, fighting and festering in the trenches….I felt a deserter.' Survivor's guilt was taking hold. 'All the times I was in hospital, every day of my voyage home, and for weeks after that, my spirit seemed to fret and chafe in the trenches, strive and sweat in the firing-lines that I knew so well. You can carry a no-longer-fit soldier's body out of the firing-line, but not his soul.'

Many decades later, a former private in the Lancashire Fusiliers wrote of Gallipoli: 'No artist can ever recapture the smell of decay – the frightening stench of corruption borne towards us on the morning breeze…[yet] this bloody place of Gallipoli fascinated you. There was a "feel" about this place that was sort of special.' Many veterans echoed this man's view; many would make the pilgrimage back to Turkey even into the 1990s. The rocky, hot, unforgiving Peninsula excited the erstwhile soldier's imagination, whether it was a sense of history repeating itself – the ruins of Troy are just a few miles away – or the simple beauty of the land fringed on all sides by the blue Aegean sea. Undoubtedly, for all, there was the memory of those who died and remained there, and a memory of collective suffering. As an officer of the Highland Light Infantry would write: 'No man was sorry to leave Gallipoli but few were really glad.' As Mure recovered, Gallipoli remained close by. '…It seems to me that Gallipoli was but yesterday.

And often the street I am on, in Edinburgh, in London, or in Paris, seems less real to me than the broken goat-paths of Gallipoli.'

It is not clear precisely when Mure wrote his memoir. The book was published in 1919 so that, at the very most, he consigned his thoughts to paper three years after the events, soon enough for memories to remain almost tangible. And yet while Mure's clarity of recall is astonishing, his experiences created an emotional sediment that clouded his own judgment as to the wider value of the campaign and its execution. That sediment had not settled sufficiently for him to divorce the everyday heroism that he witnessed by those under his command from the manifest truth that the Gallipoli campaign was lost, the Allies defeated. He dedicated his memoirs to General Sir Ian Hamilton, the much-maligned General Officer Commanding the Mediterranean Expeditionary Force, a man who badly failed in his command and was eventually replaced.

Mure ends the book by maintaining that the men who fought had left the Peninsula of their own volition. 'We left,' he wrote, 'because we wished to leave. Our landing was a triumph; our going was a triumph.' He had not been on the Gallipoli Peninsula when the fighting ceased; he had not witnessed for himself how utterly untenable was the Allied position so that evacuation was the only sensible course of action. The evacuation was a triumph only inasmuch as it was conducted with great preparation and skill, but the fact remained that the Alllies *had* to leave. It is perhaps indicative of his love for his men that he was unable, at least in 1919, to admit that their lives had been wasted on Gallipoli.

Albert Haye Mure was born in 1879 in Renfrewshire, Scotland and was commissioned into the Army in 1905. In1908 he married Ethel Forbes Lindsay and they had two children. Sadly, his wife died in 1916. After the war, as a Temporary Lieutenant Colonel, he commanded the 4th Reserve Battalion, The Royal Scots, settling in Edinburgh. In the early 1920s he returned to civilian life, working in finance and specializing in company liquidation. He subsequently remarried but died aged just 64 in 1943.

Richard van Emden
February 2015

Prologue

Tinkle, tinkle, tinkle, ting, ting, went the telephone.

The acting adjutant picked up the receiver.

'Hullo!'

'Is that 5th Battalion, the Royal Scots?'

'Yes, sir.'

'Headquarters, Scottish Command, speaking.'

'Yes, sir.'

'You move in forty-eight hours to Leamington to link up with the 29th Division.'

'Yes, sir.'

At last it had come.

Forty-eight hours later a battalion of over a thousand men steamed out of Edinburgh *en route* for that which had already been called 'The Great Adventure'. Little did one reckon that it was destined to take part in one of the most glorious chapters in our military history. Little did those who entrained that day, or those dear ones left behind to bear the agonising suspense of waiting, think how few would meet again this side of the veil.

Chapter 1

At Sea

Arriving at a dock in a troop-train at 1 a.m. on a beastly night in March is not conducive to good temper. But the experience had its points, and to most of us the novelty more than made up for all its little disagreeablenesses. But I still think (as I have thought for years) that the calendar would be greatly improved if we were to leave the month of March out of it. It's an unmannerly month.

Our boat was a liner. I have not often gone down to the sea in ships. Hitherto my sole experience of boats had been in crossing to or from Ireland, a brief but most justly celebrated form of sea-voyage, a voyage of which I invariably spent the first half fearing I was going to die, and the last half fearing I was not. Naturally, to me, who had known only the little packets of the Irish Channel, this sea-going liner seemed huge.

Leaving my second in command to look after the company, I went on board to see where my men should go. The big boat was cold – clammy cold – and the big boat was dark; and its interior seemed an endless network of low, narrow passages, all crossing and recrossing each other repeatedly, and all leading nowhere. I should say that 99 per cent of that boat's crew were asleep, and 1 per cent nowhere in particular. When I came to think of it calmly, the crew were in their proper place at that hour in the morning, especially as we were not expected to come on board until six. But at the time it struck me as inhospitable, and I felt alone and neglected.

At long last I unearthed – or should I say 'undecked'? – a quartermaster, a comfortable creature who listened to me kindly, and then said that if I'd get my men, in single file, to a certain spot (I don't remember what he called it – ships will never be my strong point), hammocks would be issued in precisely ten minutes. I said that I would do so. He kept his word, and I kept mine. Companies may have been moved more prettily, but few, I think, more quickly, than I moved mine, in the dark on that nasty March night, from slushy dock to slippery deck.

I left my senior subaltern to superintendent the actual issuing of the hammocks, and went myself to find out, if I could, what quarters had been allotted to my men. I descended, almost without mishap, sundry flights of perpendicular and spiral stairs, and again penetrated the various catacombs below.

The liner was, of course, now fitted up as a troop-ship. The five decks where cargo would be in normal times were full of long, narrow tables and forms; and from the roofs hung a battalion of big screwed-in hooks on which hammocks were to be fastened close in taut bundles by day, and to dangle soporifically at night.

The ship suddenly became a straining, struggling, man-and-hammock-infested scrum. I had never seen anything at all like it before. I have since. But I do not care how infrequently I repeat the experience.

The entire battalion had now detrained, and other company officers were in evidence with their men behind them. Officers and men came on board. That quartermaster was perfectly impartial. He issued hammocks to all comers alike, and, as far as possible, to all at once. The great ship's highways and byways became a seething tangle of hammock-bearing men, all going in different directions, and doing it vigorously.

A game now commenced which might be called 'Shove and Push.' The rules of the game were very elastic. If two men going upstairs with hammocks met two men going downstairs with hammocks, what was the rule? I don't know what the rule was, but the result depended upon which of the groups of two suddenly became a group of four, or, in military parlance, whose 'supports' arrived first. During the warmer phases of the game some of the hammocks were half in their assignees' arms, half on the floor or stairs. This added variety to the play, and gave it spicy handicap, but it was detrimental to the hammocks. One company commander at least discovered this to his cost at the end of the voyage.

I eventually found where my men were to go, but another company had mistaken their pitch, and had to evacuate first. That was quite in order, because the referee of the game had got lost, and therefore the game could not stop. Well, there is one bit of sound advice I can offer: if ever you play this game at two in the morning, never lose your temper. It is fatal.

The game gradually ceased by dint of attrition, and I discovered that I had half my company right up in the bows or forecastle. The other half were practically next door (that's not a nautical expression, but it will have to do). I had had no luck in the game – though lots of fun. If you had been in that forecastle our third day out, you would have enjoyed yourself, subject to being a sailor. I am not. A number of the men were not.

Having discovered my company's quarters, and herded the men into them, it struck me that I had been working hard, and without 'supports'. I had my men settled. But where were my subalterns? None was to be seen. I threaded the passages; I climbed the ladders. At last I discovered two of my aides – but no sign of the other two. They were not with my second in command. So I made tracks for the official quarters. These were easy to find, and on going along the corridor I saw that the name of each officer, clearly written, had been tacked on the door of the cabin he was to occupy. That quartermaster deserves to be 'mentioned'.

I discovered my own cabin, and then went in search of those of my subalterns. I found one with the names of the two boys I was hunting on its door. Well, probably I'd find them sometime, and in the meantime I might as well see how they were quartered, and if everything was nice and pretty for them – flowers on the dressing-table and plenty of logs on the fire. I went in. That was my moment of greatest astonishment. The cabin was occupied. Its owners were in bed, fast asleep.

Then there was trouble! It was three in the morning. My temper had been severely taxed for hours. I am quite sure those boys had never dressed so quickly before in their fives. *I* went to bed.

Next morning they both apologised humbly. Having had a splendid bath and an excellent breakfast, and feeling human once more, I reminded them of a certain 'para.' in the Manual and closed the incident.

Poor boys! One has made 'the supreme sacrifice', and the other is out of the service, wounded in action too severely to fight again.

The next day we spent in settling down; and the other regiment who were shipping with us came on board. They had one-half of the ship, and we the other. That night at dinner some one said suddenly, 'We're off!' and so we were. Our momentous voyage had begun.

At ten every morning we had 'Ship's Rounds', a very earnest function. The captain, an absolute monarch, the two commanding officers, the adjutants, the sergeant-majors, the captain of the day, and various smaller fry went round and inspected the whole ship, barring the engine-room. It was a very minute inspection, and usually the adjutants collected a wonderful fund of information, which later on they dished up to various responsible persons, sometimes as a savoury, sometimes not.

I went round very minutely myself our first morning, going to the forecastle and inspecting my own men's quarters before the general inspection. I had ten messes right in the bows, three decks down; and I couldn't go any farther 'for'ard' unless I went out with the anchor.

There was a sergeant who did nothing else but look after the company's quarters. I picked him out for the job more by chance than anything else. It was a lucky leap in the dark. He was never once 'sick'. Why he wasn't and how he wasn't I don't know, for the scenes he must have witnessed beggar description.

The third day out was our test of good or bad sailorship. After 'Rounds' we usually had 'Physical Exercise'. This soon after a big breakfast, at sea at least, is not always conducive to comfort. Now, in the army seasickness is not a disease, nor yet an illness. And unless you are ill you must go on parade. Fortunately for me, my mind triumphed over my body, but it was a near thing. Not always was every one else as lucky; but then the men soon got their sea-legs, and ere long every one started to enjoy himself. The other regiment had just come from India (via the Bay of Biscay), and were hardened.

Our third or fourth day out one of my men was found asleep while on sentry duty beside the water-tank. This was a very serious crime. He had to be brought before the C.O. for punishment. I ordered the company sergeant-major to have the prisoner at Orderly-Room in plenty of time. Having every confidence in my C.S.M., I myself 'rolled up' (the ship was rolling too) at the last moment. To my horror, there was neither sergeant-major, escort, nor prisoner present. I got hold of two of my men and sent them to hunt for the delinquents. They were not to be found. Orderly-Room time had passed. I went in, hardly able to keep my feet, but lurching as little as I could, and faced the adjutant. He cursed roundly, and I could say nothing, as I was the officer responsible. At that moment the sergeant-major *staggered* in – violently seasick. The escort and the prisoner had succumbed to the same malady, infected perhaps by the sight and other signs of his torture, and had disappeared. They were found half-an-hour later in a horrible plight. I had to put my sergeant-major under arrest; I was ordered to do so. This was his first default in over twenty years of service, and the next day he was admonished. I think he felt it. I know I did. I felt it bitterly, and felt that I was to blame. Officially there is no such thing as seasickness in the British forces. Assuredly discipline must be maintained – and should be. But the red-tape that takes no account of seasickness, one of the acutest discomforts the human body can know, seems to need cutting.

Our first stop was at Malta. Few of my men had been abroad before; their interest was immense, and their comments were vastly original.

We left the next morning. No one knew where we were going. But every one thought he did, and I certainly heard a hundred or more places proclaimed in confidence as our destination. About two days out from Malta, Alexandria became hot favourite in the betting.

The voyage through the Mediterranean was delightful. We got to know well the officers of the other regiment aboard. I had wondered just how 'Regulars' would regard us. These officers were charming. Most of them had had many years' experience, and without exception they seemed eager to bestow (but never to impose) any advice and information they could on an amateur like myself. I shall always remember one thing that one of them, Major Summat, 1st Essex, said to me: 'My boy, you are a soldier now, and are going into the real thing.' I have remembered that sentence on more occasions than one.

It soon became an open secret that it was Alexandria that we were making for, and on 2 April 1915, we arrived there.

Chapter 2

A Little Nearer

In Egypt the 5th Royal Scots trained for nine days, and then left in three portions for the next stage.

In war-time the British soldier is well shepherded. All that can be done for his comfort and convenience is done, and done cordially. The officer must fend for himself a dozen times a day, which is all as it should be. I had very much to fend for myself when I reached the quay the day we left Alexandria. Finding our particular boat (her identification disc was not conspicuous) was rather a hunt-the-thimble sort of business in the crowded harbour *mêlée*. But at last I found it.

Seeing no signs of life on deck, I left my men 'at ease' on the quay, and boarded (or bearded) the vessel alone. Roaming the deck, I discovered an individual in shirt-sleeves looking down upon me from a dark and perilous perch. At least, it appeared perilous to me. I inquired for the master (I believe that is the correct term for the skipper of such craft, but I usually said 'captain' – it came more naturally). He of the shirt-sleeves said that he was the master, and added, 'Come along up the ladder'. I went up the ladder. Before my foot was off the top rung the master threw at my head, 'Will you have a whisky-and-soda?' From that moment I called the coatless one a gentleman. And so, indeed, he proved – a real treasure of the deep. There are many such afloat under the Union Jack, and some of them in queer-looking boats.

Captain King was a charming chap. He made light of all war's troubles, and of its perils nothing at all. Like most sailors, he had an unshakable faith in premonitions and in foresigns. He *knew* that he was predestined to die at home, on his bed, in the most orderly and orthodox manner. And this was quite a comfort, as there were rumours, and more than rumours, of enemy submarines in near waters.

While I drank my whisky the master stood and shook his head at me. 'Have another! Oh yes, but do, for you've no business here – so drink to it. You've no right to arrive so soon. I've had no instructions to take you on, or about you at all.' I produced my 'instructions', and, seeing that we were otherwise houseless and homeless, he consented to accept them in lieu of his own, and the men were allowed on board. That skipper was one of the very best. The steward was also a good sort, and almost before the last man was up and over the gang-plank, he had an excellent meal served out for them – piping hot, well cooked, abundant, and clean. It wasn't a liner, this second ship of ours, but it was a most 'comfy' boat, more home-like than I could have believed that a boat could be, and we settled down, grateful and glad.

In the morning an ammunition column of R.F.A. arrived, and I divided my detachment into fatigue-parties to help in loading. Forage and stores began to arrive also, and we were more than comfortably busy.

Next day the divisional ammunition column commander came with a few of his men and no end of munitions. My detachment consisted of about one hundred men of 'all sorts' – artists, students, clerks, tradesmen, skilled business men, etc, from Scotland. It was splendid to see how, without exception, they adapted themselves to these hard and bustling circumstances. Nothing seemed too stiff or too dirty.

The derricks were the stumbling-block in the proceedings. But I had a lance-corporal who had been a marine and, as '*Ubique*' is the marines' motto, he took charge of derrick fatigues with a will and a rush. Under him the men played with that heavy ammunition – the heavier it was, the harder they played. They used to fling shell ammunition about in a way that would, I should think, have given a munition-factory foreman cerebrospinal meningitis. Yet nothing happened. The 'stores' they treated with more respect. If I remember rightly, one box of biscuits slipped to a salt and watery grave in the harbour. But not a drop of the rum ration was spilled or mislaid; the very greatest care was taken of the rum ration.

Our transport and officers' chargers had come, so far, from England in other boats than ours. They linked up with us now. As I stood leaning on the rail, watching the loading and taking long last looks at Egypt, who should come walking down the quay but my own dainty dancer – the brute – led by his groom! I refused to recognise or claim the beast, but told the groom to let me know when the horrid quadruped was going to be slung on board. I wished to stand by and jeer at him. On my first day in the glory of O.C. Company, he had made me the laughing-stock of a regiment. I would curse him and gibe at him before the tombs of all the Ptolemies, in the very presence of the Sphinx, witnessed by as much of the British Army as was assembled together there on the Alexandrian quay. I did think of bribing the derrick Tommy to drop him hard, but it didn't seem quite sporting to treat him so, for was not he, as well as I, faring forth, perhaps to die; and in the same great cause, for the same Greater Britain? As a matter of fact he came aboard gracefully, and got safely into his stall in the hold.

It was great fun watching the mules being shipped. You might have thought some had lived their lives in slings. Others had a rooted aversion to them. The saying 'as stubborn as a mule' is a true saying. But I was convinced that some of these were proud, rather than stubborn. Some held up their head and looked truly martial. Some cocked an ear and held their head sideways, for all the world like a terrier pup. Some were jaunty; some wept aloud. Some waved a humorous leg, and some an angry one. Some took it stoically, some all in good part, some in the worst possible spirit and taste. They lacked *esprit de corps*, those army mules *en route* to Gallipoli. They had no uniform standard of conduct or of carriage.

It was a 'top-hole' voyage. We were a merry mess of eight officers, four of whom were Regulars. The O.C. troops was a gunner. The adjutant, Lieutenant W. D. Hislop, a clever artist, was one of my subalterns. Though our boat was a 'tramp' (I apologise to the captain, if ever he reads this and recognises his ship), personally I enjoyed the voyage much better than I had that on the liner. The men also were very much more comfortable. They had sports every day and singsongs every night, and were as jolly and contented a lot as you could wish to see.

On the forenoon we were sailing a mail arrived. Home letters! This was just the one thing needed to enhance our already very high spirits. I know how eagerly letters from 'the front' are coveted and read and kept at 'home'. But I think that home letters are even more to us at the front. How much they are their writers can scarcely suspect. There is no telling it.

Just before we cast off, one of my men came to me, anxious and hurried, with a War Office letter requesting him to report at Nigg, Ross-shire, Scotland, he having been given a commission. The letter had just missed him before his going overseas, and had been chasing him ever since. There was little time to think it over and decide what should be done. I suppose, technically, he ought to have left us then and there, and found his way back to Scotland. But he begged to stay with the company, now so near the fighting-line. I agreed, and promised to lay the little tangle before the C.O. when we linked up again with the regiment. I fancied the C.O. would attach him as an officer, pending Whitehall instructions as to his disposal. And to take him with us seemed the sane, as well as the kind, thing to do, as, should he go back to Scotland, by the time he got there he almost certainly would find that his regiment was in some other and far-distant theatre of war, and would have to spend the rest of the war chasing it about the globe – chasing always, but never quite catching up. 'I came out to see this show, and I want to see it first at any rate,' he pleaded, far keener to get into the fight than to take up his commission. Before instructions about him reached us he was wounded and sent back to hospital at Alexandria. Through an error he was reported in the casualty list as killed, and read of his own death in papers sent to Egypt to him from home. A number of soldiers do that. When this one was well again he came back to the peninsula as an officer, and there, alas! fell gallantly leading his men.

We sailed in the early forenoon, escorted (as we were all the way) by T.B.D.'s, for submarines were all about us on the voyage. A second transport started at the same time with another of our detachments. This was a much faster boat than ours, and soon left us behind and out of sight. But the race is not always to the swift, especially in war, and we reached Gallipoli before she did! For two days the men had a nice, lazy time. With the exception of just enough physical exercise to keep them in training, we gave them no work, as they had been working more than hard for some time now. The better the soldier, the wiser and the more necessary it is to let (or, if need be, make) him rest now and then. Like every other fine instrument, he loses his edge and his power if not laid on a shelf to rest from time to time. All that our men had to do now most of the time was to watch the gunners at stables and exercising their horses. It is wonderful how you can exercise a horse on board ship, and well worth seeing. Watching it one day, I thought of my own animal, and, relenting, went down to the hold to see it. I took a pocketful of lump-sugar with me. But it would have none of me, nor a lump of my offering. A pretty, friendly mare in the next stall got the benefit of my dancer's evil temper. I know that beast hated me. I never saw it again – nor wished to.

Our third day out, at one in the morning, of all unkind hours, I was rudely waked by a voice shouting through a megaphone, 'What ship is this?' I immediately pictured a fleet of enemy submarines, and thought grimly of all the ammunition in the hold, and what a rotten end it might be to our Mediterranean errand. I climbed out of my berth and took a look through my port-hole. I saw one of our own destroyers. It was a comforting sight. It lay very close to us – so close that it seemed as if I might almost touch it. I heard the commander give an order to change our course several degrees, and then I curled up again to complete my interrupted repose. I was very sleepy – one usually is at sea – and at that ungodly hour was not particularly interested to know why we were changing our course.

We had an event on board ship the next morning, an addition to the strength of the ship's company arriving in the shape of a foal. The mother lived all right, but the little raw recruit stayed but a day. It was a pretty beastie, and every one of us was sorry when it died.

A little later, when we had almost reached our destination – Mudros Bay, as we all knew now (though to quite a few of us that didn't mean as much as it might have done) – we spied a ship on the horizon. She turned out to be the faster transport, which, with one of our detachments aboard, had left Alexandria when we did. We beat her by a short head going into the bay, much to our delight. We cheered as if we'd whipped the Turks. There are no greater children than British soldiers on active service – between the volleys – except British soldiers afloat. The changing of our course to avoid submarines had saved us a great many miles. Our old craft sailed into Mudros Bay as slowly and as leisurely as she had sailed away from Egypt. But still we cheered and cheered and cheered, officers as well as men. We were all boys together on many of those taut, grim, early days. We dropped anchor in the outer harbour.

Chapter 3

Mudros Bay

As we came on deck the next morning a wonderful sight met the eye. Our ship was one of the farthest out, and on our looking up-harbour towards Lemnos, a veritable forest of masts could be seen. Slightly on our starboard side the stately H.M.S. *Queen Elizabeth* (or '*Lizzie*', as she was familiarly called) rode at anchor, for the time being not belching forth her deadly missiles of destruction. Ahead of us was H.M.T.S. *Southland*, a large liner. Ahead again, developing into a huge fan-like shape, were craft of all descriptions – battleships, cruisers, T.B.D.'s, mine-sweepers, liners, tramps, colliers, paddle-steamers, down to a felucca slipping along in the breeze, its owner watching with Greek cunning his chance of selling the fruit piled up in the bow. The only blot in the landscape – or, rather, the heavens – was a Hun plane at a high altitude, evidently out for reconnaissance work.

Here on their transports were the 29th Division, ready for the fray; and though much has been said of this famous division, the reader will, I hope, pardon my digressing for a page or two in order to pay tribute in passing to its soldierly qualities.

The division was composed of troops of the same standing and calibre as the original British Expeditionary Force, with the exception of the divisional Signal Company, the Argyll and Bute Mountain Battery, and the 5th Battalion, the Royal Scots. These were Territorials.

The Royal Scots, as we have seen, had had the privilege of coming out from the Old Country on H.M.T.S. *Caledonia* (a Clan liner, commanded by Captain Blaikie, who was taken prisoner later when his ship was torpedoed) along with the 1st Essex. The 1st Essex were magnificent men, tall, well built, and trained to the moment. We looked like pigmies in comparison, and rumour had it that the Territorials would probably be used as hewers of wood and haulers of water. It was a natural assumption on the part of men who had been on duty abroad for years, and most of whom, officers included, had never seen a Territorial. But still it was consoling to us Territorials to think that both the water and the wood were necessary to enable our Regulars to fight. The greatest compliment I was ever paid was a month later when their adjutant (Captain Wood, since killed) came up to me one day, shook hands, and said, 'Mure, I should be damned proud to lead your men anywhere.' I felt indeed proud myself.

On the peninsula we fought practically the whole time side by side with our shipmates, and soon got to know one another after our natural Scottish shyness had worn off! On board the *Caledonia* was also the headquarters staff of the 88th Brigade, in which brigade we were. General Napier and the brigade major were killed when landing from the *River Clyde*, the staff captain escaping (Captain Sinclair Thomson, 1st Essex, later general staff officer, 1st grade). They were charming and courteous, and though rather overawed when addressed by a 'brass hat', you were soon put at your ease. During the war it has been my good fortune, perhaps more than most Territorial officers, to work with Regular officers of the old school, and I can only say that I have always met with the greatest courtesy and kindness, together with an unfailing desire to help an amateur in acquiring the necessary knowledge in the 'art of war' which only comes by experience.

The present day Socialist, or whatever he calls himself, may decry the army, but if a battalion, band at its head, marched past his home, I am certain he would get up from his fireside and watch it passing. The law of order and discipline cannot be got over, just as the law of supply and demand is inexorable. It is a well-known fact that the Australians were, at the beginning, slack in saluting (I mean no disparagement to our friends from the Antipodes, as discipline is not instilled into a being in a day or a month), but a 29th Division officer was always saluted by them – not, perhaps, from the routine of drill, but from respect for their fighting qualities. And this, I venture to say, was a high compliment from these grim, determined, fearless soldiers. It was a sort of Masonic hallmark given by them to a division whose conduct they had witnessed and approved.

All that the '29th' did and endured in Gallipoli may never be told. What it lost is numbered and recorded, and its part from the beginning to the end of the war, if ever chronicled, will be found second to none.

One might write much more, but to return to our story.

A week's hard training had now to be gone in for – training in descending and ascending rope ladders dangling over the ship's side into lighters. This was no easy matter in full marching order, but it had also its humorous side. To me it wasn't particularly funny, because the rifles of the men were in my charge, and though you can fish a man out of the water, a rifle is not so obliging as to give you the chance. We had gunners also on board who did not participate in this form of amusement, but they were not to be done out of their share, which consisted usually in throwing the manure over the side where the ladder was. Even the cooks had to have their look in with the slops.

It is said that we Britons are not facile, that we learn with difficulty, and adapt ourselves to new conditions and circumstances badly. Well, it is not true of British soldiers; nothing could be less true.

After a few days my secret orders came, telling me what to do after we had unloaded, and where to go. Excitement began to run high. The air commenced to tingle, and though you couldn't see it, you could feel that a great commotion was going on in the inner harbour.

On April 24, about five o'clock, the cruisers, their decks crowded with troops, started to pass us. One cruiser, I noticed, was packed with Australian troops, a magnificent body of men. Mudros harbour may not have looked like Sydney harbour, but it had elements of wide space and active emergency, probably more welcome to them and more appropriate than the Bakerloo tube, a Clapham side-street, or the purlieus of Tottenham Court Road. They appeared splendid; they were splendid; and with the ships' bands playing, they were radiant with high spirits and enthusiasm.

It must not be thought that they took the enterprise lightly. Every man there realised its momentousness and its terrible tragedy. They were young gladiators, stripped for one of the biggest fights the world has yet seen. They were exultant because they were brave, and because they were proud of their cause, not because they were for one moment foolhardy. They knew their danger, and they mocked at it. They knew their peril, and they jeered at it. They knew the odds against them, and they didn't give a damn. We cheered them with a will, and they cheered back mightily. It was to be the first battle of a young and puissant people, giants girded and exultant. I don't know how it made them feel, but their eyes were primed and their faces glowing. It made me feel that at last we were going to do something, and that Melbourne, Edinburgh, Glasgow, Hobart were all Homeland – ours –

and that they and we were closest of kin, 'Jock Tamson's bairns', every mother's son of us.

Then our ship came. Not the tramp I was on, but the liner carrying my battalion. Ah, how we cheered them!

That evening we ourselves received sailing orders for 6 a.m. the next morning.

Chapter 4

The Start of the Great Adventure

We left sharp on time, and at last our 'Great Adventure' began, as the day of 25 April dawned.

Cape Helles is the southernmost point of Gallipoli peninsula, and it was there and in its vicinity that we of the 29th Division and the men of the Royal Naval Division were to land. The three principal landings were to be made at Cape Helles itself – at Beach V, Beach W, and Beach X. Other landings were to be accomplished at Beaches S and Y and near Gaba Tepe.

The 5th Royal Scots were originally intended to land at V Beach in support of the Dublins, Munsters, and Hampshires. Owing to the attack here being held up, however, the 'Royals' were diverted to Beach W – the 'Lancashire landing', as it came to be called – which lay between V and X. Personally I doubt if there was much to choose among the three. None of them was a health-resort or a garden of roses. W was a narrow patch of sand between a diminutive bay and cliffs and strong entrenchments. The Turks had it well watched and warded; machine-guns, barbed wire, and mines defended the cliff and the bay.

After sailing for about an hour and a half we heard a faint boom, and then another. Excitement began to permeate the troops, and even the ship's company officers (with whom callous calm was an ambition and an obsession) began to show an active interest in things in general, and in the sounds from Gallipoli in particular. Officers young and old began to come on deck quickly, and breakfast was forgotten.

I must have been standing by the side of the bridge watching, listening, *thinking,* for some time, when Captain John Wilson, my second in command, hailed me. John is a thorough Scotsman. He did not refer to the reverberant action, but remarked, 'Weel, Mure, I think we micht hae a wee bit bite. It may be some time afore we get anither, and an empty stummic's no guid for ony mom.' I agreed, and we went down off the bridge and had a 'rare guid tuck in.'

The booming became more intense and more rapid, and as we returned to the deck we saw a flash. And now flash followed flash, quick upon each other's heels, and thick as woes in Elsinore.

The end of the peninsula came in sight, grey, uninviting, fringed with a mighty fleet – battleships, transports, and craft of every conceivable kind. As we steamed slowly to our allotted anchorage, well in to the shore, the sight was worth all the fatigue, all the work, all the peril and the misery that came after.

We anchored close to a huge cruiser, and as she belched her broadsides at the Turk our little boat trembled and shook from bow to stern. We were too close, and at dusk had to move a bit farther out. When we had done so, the little craft actually seemed grateful!

But that was after I had spent a wonderful hour on the bridge, and watched the battle. I had a good telescope, its loan one of the captain's hundred kindnesses. I saw splendidly.

The fleet was bombarding the Asiatic side, where the French were drawing Turkish fire by making a feint of landing. On that side there was a long cliff with the usual row of Eastern houses on the top. It was extraordinary to see a house crumple and topple down. The Russian battleship, with its five funnels, christened by Tommy the

'Packet of Woodbines', did great execution. One felt like cheering every time a house crashed down or a fire started. What looked to be a cottage was built on a small promontory jutting out from the edge of the cliff. For hours the little building defied the gunners, and seemed almost to mock the best marksmanship in Europe, so long did it stand unscathed. At last a shell landed right into it, and down it came at the first touch, exactly like a castle of playing-cards, such as you and I used to build – years ago. The whole ship cheered vociferously. I am afraid the officers had had a 'wee bit gamble' on that poor little house; but, we being Scots, nobody made a book. Its end was unmistakable. When it had toppled to its doom, we turned our attention to graver matters of battle. Krithia, well to our north, was ablaze, and Achi Baba, just beyond, was getting a generous share of the 'heavies'.

We could not tell how the day was going. Indescribable noise we could hear, indescribable flame and confusion we could see, indescribable carnage we could infer, but we could not piece together or interpret the awful confusion of detail. There was a green field to the left on the top of the cliff, and we could see men rushing across it, then coming back, then advancing again, as if a stiff fight were going on. Towards Sedd-el-Bahr there seemed to be no progress, and we, watching and waiting, began to feel nervous, and imagined that all was not well.

Wilson suddenly turned to me and said, 'There are the stretcher cases going aboard the hospital ship. Some poor devils have got it in the neck already.' Of course, a great many had – we knew that – but this was seeing it.

We little guessed what was happening on the beaches. A pinnace dashed past us, and we yelled to the officer. He shook his head, and that finished us. Anxiety turned into absolute, craven dumps. I suddenly realised that I was very hungry. I looked at my watch. It was very much tea-time, and lunch had been quite forgotten. We made dejectedly for the modest cabin, which the captain's partiality and our good manners termed 'the saloon'. There we ate and drank, almost in silence. But, in spite of our long fast, a very little satisfied us, and we filed back on deck as dejectedly as we had filed down.

It was evident by this time that a landing had been effected, though not so successful a landing as had been anticipated. But we had begun. We were doing something – the rattle of musketry told that. It became more pronounced as the evening wore on, sharper, quicker, more distraught, as if thousands of death-dice were being tossed feverishly by the nervous hands of a multitude of desperate gamblers.

I don't think many slept that night, and sharp at dawn every man of us was up and astir to see – if he could – what was happening. It was then that we got our baptism of fire, and broke together the red communion bread of imminent, deadly peril, as a shell from the Asiatic side squelched into the water near us, and in an instant another, so close that it almost touched us. Scores of them had rocketed over us for the last half-hour, but until then none had come or seemed very near. It is remarkable how soon, in actual battle, one grows to take little or no account of the missiles that scurry over one, no matter how deadly one knows them to be – we learned that war lesson almost at once, in less than an hour; but never can one get inured or indifferent to the grim, reverberating reminder of a great shell bursting close at hand.

An hour later, thralled and breathless, I was watching the first big infantry charge I had ever seen. It was a glorious and a terrible sight, and I felt as it looked – fearful and exultant. The infantry pushed and tore through the village of Sedd-el-Bahr up to the fort belching fire and death from the cliff beyond. The blood danced in our veins, as we leaned and looked, our souls fighting with those men struggling in the thick of the carnage. Their bayonets flashed in the dancing eastern sunlight, and as the men rattled on, bleeding, dying, yet persisting, conquering, the glittering sheen they threw before them and about them scintillated like a sea of liquid, burnished steel, more alive than the molten sunlight it mocked and outshone, throwing great swathes of terrible searchlight for yards in front of our straining, suffering infantry, and for yards on either side of them. It was a field of the cloth of living silver. And we could hear the men shouting, 'Go on, lads; go on, you devils! Give them hell!' and cries much more vitriolic, less episcopal. 'Go on, lads' – nothing very Homeric in that! Ah! wait and hear – hear it from a thousand British throats when the day runs red and the fight rises and falls in awful sheets and sweeps of torture and slaughter, necks knotted, backs strained, eyes and hearts bursting, breasts heaving and panting, wounds unheeded, death mocked and defied.

The fort was taken. We saw our men stagger and sway with fatigue and the recoil of mighty work done and accomplished. Then they recovered, threw off their brief relaxation (it had been but an instant), shook themselves into position, and re-formed. It was the second of our Gallipoli victories, but the cost was bitter and dear, as the victories of war must almost always be. Lieutenant-Colonel Doughty-Wylie of the General Staff had gone ashore to direct operations. He had to lead the assault, and leading, he fell, just when the fort was as good as taken. And for a monument to a man and a soldier the fort was given his name.

In the afternoon we received a signal that ammunition was needed, and presently a pinnace came along with a lighter in tow. Then there was turmoil. Every officer itched and clamoured to go. But O.C. troops was on board, and he went himself, and took my second in command with him. I silently consigned them both to a place which, after all, was probably cool and comfortable compared with the spot where they landed.

They both came back safely towards sunset, and we gathered about them like schoolboys round a toffee-box. But they wouldn't talk. I believe they couldn't. Wilson said that 'it was indescribable', and that was every word that I could get out of him.

About 1 a.m. next morning still more ammunition was wanted, and my chance had come.

Chapter 5

The Landing at V Beach

I SET off in a pinnace towing two ammunition lighters, and headed for the *River Clyde*, an old collier that had been turned into a sort of ferry-boat for troops, to carry them from troopship to shore. Great open spaces had been cut in her side at her between-decks, and lower down platforms and runs had been built that men might rush from her quickly when landing under accurate fire. Encased machine-guns stood on her forecastle that she might, when desirable, give the Turks fire for fire. She had now been beached, purposely, as near shore as had been found practicable. From her to the shore ran a rough bridge of boats, lighters, and miscellaneous small craft across which the men had to crawl and slide to the shore. This bridge had been built at a terrible cost, with a disregard of death as glorious as anything in the history of war. When the *River Clyde* was beached twenty-five launches packed with men slipped ahead of her, and the men in them – knowing perfectly the nature and the extent of their danger – began to make the required bridge, getting small boats into position and securely moored, working from the *River Clyde* to the beach. Soon after she grounded, the Turks opened fire on the heroic little bridge of boats, finished half-way or more to the shore, bombarding it from the ruined castle of Sedd-el-Bahr, from the higher town, and from the splendidly fortified and magnificently manned and munitioned hill that stretched across the bay, aiming at a target that even poor marksmen could not have missed – and these were good marksmen. The waiting troops on the big ship were more protected, for the *River Clyde* was fortified too, and had many contrivances of defence, but the little boats were naked and helpless. The Turks are computed to have sent from five to twelve thousand shots a minute into that devoted band of men. Not one man flinched. But most of them died. As a boatload perished, men rushed down the gangway of the *Clyde* and carried on. A man who lived ten minutes under that Turkish fire seemed to have a charmed life. Most dropped within four minutes. But before they dropped they worked – ah, how they worked while they yet lived! Each did his small vital bit; and when he lurched bleeding into his sea-grave, a comrade, newly come, snatched up his job until he too died, to be succeeded by yet another British soldier. The men waiting on the collier, silent for the most part, but some swearing, fought among themselves to be the next to go. The holocaust was hideous, but the object for which the men died was fulfilled. The bridge was completed, and the Turks could not prevent it. A Turkish officer, our prisoner later, swore by Allah that it was the finest thing he ever saw, and ten times braver than he would have credited of any man, Christian or Mussulman. It was over this blood-cemented bridge that Lieutenant-Colonel Doughty-Wylie had led his men, to storm, through indescribable difficulties, the ruins of Sedd-el-Bahr. And it was over it that I now went, as cautiously as possible, leaving my pinnace beside the *River Clyde,* and scrambling as best I could from boat to boat. The moon had risen by this time, and the beastly evidences of the relentless conflict were thick about; you could not fail to see them clearly, and they looked all the ghastlier in the theatrical limelight of the Orient moon. The heroism of the troops who built that bridge of boats, in daylight, under tremendous, hellish fire, must have been superlative. It beggars all words, and I will attempt none. But we thought of them, and our thoughts were eloquent. For we found it no small tiring to pick our way, at our own pace, the Turks temporarily inactive, over those swaying, bobbing craft. To go over them in full marching order must have been a difficult feat in itself, let alone building the way as they went, doing it under shot and shell raining down at the rate of ten thousand shots a minute.

On reaching the beach, I clambered over the lighters to see where the ammunition was to be dumped first, and began to slip and slide all over the place. I bent down to examine the wood on which I was skidding, and I saw – well, it wasn't water that was making me slide about! It was something thicker than water.

On the shore I found a very tired-looking assistant-beachmaster. He seemed 'all in', but he directed me alertly enough where to go and what to do. Nothing in all my brief but vigorous soldiering has impressed me more than the miraculous way in which men who look completely finished can and do go on, not only doggedly (that one expects, of course, until they drop), but vigorously and alertly. I remarked to the assistant-beachmaster, 'You seem to have had a pretty thick time.' He answered not a word. He only looked at me. It was enough. I shall remember that look while I live. There were words, and more than words, in his eyes. They seemed to say, 'I'd far rather suffer the tortures of the damned than go through *that* again.' I turned and went away quietly, rather sheepishly, I suspect, back over the lighters to my pinnace to give the necessary orders, thinking hard the while. One does a good deal of vivid thinking in one's first days of actual warfare. As time goes on one's senses get blunted for the time being; but it all comes back sharply enough afterwards. It is Providence, I take it, that steps in and does the temporary blunting; otherwise mortal men could not carry on.

Commanding the pinnace was a midshipman of His Majesty's Navy, a 'snotty'. I really think these boys – you can call them nothing else – are the bravest of all Britain's brave. Certainly they are second to none. Among all the branches of our services that I have worked with, I have never seen quite their match. Yet for the most part they are downy-faced lads, soft-skinned, warm from home and mothering. An Eton school captain told me once that he could always pick out the 'mother's boys' from any footer team, because they always gave and took the hardest kicks. And his remark often came back to me at Gallipoli. This particular boy had been at it for over seventy-two hours without a moment's rest. Impossible? Of course it was, *but he had done it.* 'In the lexicon of youth,' you know; and the Dardanelles campaign was an endless chain of impossibilities done – and done well. He had done it, and there was no look of 'all in' in his face. Merry as a cricket, he took charge of me at once. It is no exaggeration to say that he mothered me. Each time the Turks woke up a bit, he coaxed or commanded me to take cover behind the netting of sandbags which served the pinnace for earthworks, but never once would he take cover himself. It never occurred to him to do so, and when it was suggested he only laughed, and went on working and whistling. He was greatly annoyed because one of his pals had had the luck to get pinked, just a scratch somewhere – wrist, I think – and could brag he had been wounded. 'Lucky beggar!'

I admit being a trifle excited at having at last put my foot on the enemy's soil, and any number of things, no immediate part of 'my job,' escaped me. After finishing giving instructions for unloading, I noticed for the first time a continual spattering in the water beside me, not many feet away, and it dawned on me that it was bullets, a rain of bullets from the machine-guns and the rifles of the enemy on the cliff above. I was safe enough in the pinnace at the moment, for we were under the lee of the *River Clyde,* and the bullets were going over us. But they made an uncanny sound, and again I did a little thinking. It was all right enough on the pinnace, but our work there would be over presently, and it was all very wrong indeed going across the lighters to the beach. However, I was favoured with beginner's luck, and had no one hit.

Tommy is a wonderful creature! When we were on the beach my chief difficulty was to get the men to hurry up with the job, as every one of them desired to have a look round. They are as full of curiosity as monkeys are; far more curious than children, but very like children. New places drive them crazy, if they are not allowed to investigate. I had to tell them repeatedly that the war was waiting, but the Turks were not, before I could get them really to knuckle down. Not once but fifty times have I seen Tommy down arms, go up to, and gaze curiously at, a comrade whom any one from a distance of twenty yards could see had made the 'supreme sacrifice', then turn round, come slowly back, and in a surprised tone of voice say to a pal, 'Say, mate, that un's gone West!' Then the mate would give over his work, go and have a long look, come slowly back, and say, 'So he has, Bill.' *Esprit de corps!* Tommy's *esprit de corps.*

Soon after we had reached the beach I lost a man for quite a time. When at last he reappeared I 'strafed' him roundly, but his reply was too much for me. He replied, 'I'm sorry, sir; but I just wanted to see what was going on at the top of the bank.' And I had thought him killed!

About three o'clock (still a.m.) a French regiment began to disembark just beside us. They were wonderfully quiet, almost noiseless. But they looked – to me – not a little like fully dressed

Christmas-trees. They seemed to have every conceivable object slung and tied on their backs.

It was not much after four when I got back to the ship, feeling quite pleased with myself. I had done my first bit.

Chapter 6

Carrying On

We spent the next morning running horses and ammunition ashore. The gunner officer, with the D.A.C. officer, left for the beach, leaving me O.C. troops. A naval officer arrived to take charge of the ship during the unloading, and though we were being shelled fairly heavily, every one was too busy to think much about it. On active service the finest cure for being nervy is work.

We heard about noon that our half-battalion had landed on Sunday evening, and had suffered very few casualties. Not an officer had been hit.

On the 28th I was on the beach all day long, hard at it. Fighting, actual personal encounter or contribution to battle, is but one part of soldiering. The tangible brief 'fight' is the concentration of months of indescribably arduous and intricate preparation and transport, which is quite another part of soldiering. Things are thought out at home, munitions are made, stores gathered and packed, men trained and equipped. The simply enormous transport work is accomplished, no matter at what cost, over what distance. The awful goal of the imminent carnage reached, literally ten thousand indispensable, nerve-racking, back-breaking tasks confront and fatigue the soldier, who must work his hard way through them to his hour of supreme trial. The athlete pitted to run a race, the artist about to create a great role, paint a picture, achieve a masterpiece, the statesman selected to guide a realm, trains for it, feeds for it, *rests* for it. The soldier about

to plunge into the cauldron of hell that is called 'battle', with death
or torture its probable end, digs a trench that he knows may be his
own grave, shoulders crates of jam, carries unmanageable burdens of
wire and lead, harries distraught animals, washes clothes, runs here
and there on sore, blistering feet, refreshes his nerves and his eyes on
festering heaps of wounded and dead, and sleeps, if he sleep, within
sound of the guns that menace him as they slaughter the comrades
that shared his breakfast – and – and then goes 'over the top' in his
turn.

We had by this time made considerable advance both inroad on the
peninsula and in preparation of all sorts. What we had gained, how
far we had penetrated in this deadly, warded place, I knew as yet but
scantily and in disjointed scraps. News filtered through, of course, but
I had little leisure to listen. But of what the men in my immediate
charge were doing, and the splendid spirit in which they sweated on at
a job as uninteresting as it was gigantic, and as perilous as any actual
battle could be, I saw and knew all. Back and forth they waded all day
long, from the beach to the small boats, from the boats to the shore,
unloading, carrying, stacking up, sorting munitions, food, water, stores
of every sort; shells and bullets falling thick, fast, constantly. It was one
rain of death. Not a box reached the sand without being a target to the
Turk. All day long the men worked and carried and waded, walking
over the dying and the dead, when they had to. Have you ever walked
over dead men, still warm and quivering?

It was an Olympian game, and like gods the men played it. War's
awful housewifery is a service for heroes!

About four in the afternoon I had a spare hour, and felt entitled to
use it as I chose. The wounded were beginning to come down, and I
thought I'd see if I could find any of our fellows.

The organisation already started was extraordinarily perfect, and proved that the initial staff work had been thought out most carefully. The great difference between the Western front and Gallipoli may not have struck the reader. On the Western front there were all the troops in lines of communication; in Gallipoli the fighting troops had to take on this work and fight at the same time. I need say no more. Nothing seemed to have been forgotten, and in all the apparent *mêlée* and confusion of war, under all but insuperable difficulties, and under quite insuperable disadvantages, everything was working with surprising smoothness. Certainly the R.A.M.C. and hospital arrangements could not have been better under the circumstances. That under such conditions they were half so good was nothing short of a miracle.

Hospital marquees had been put up; an ordnance depot had been marked out; already salvage was being collected; and the A.S.C. was in full working order.

Whatever critics may say after the war – and of course they'll say wonderful much – it is difficult to believe that they will find anything to urge against our powers of organisation, or the devotion and the ability with which every detail of the enormous work was carried out and perfected. We are indeed an extraordinary nation. We take time, but we get there.

Eventually we do get there, in spite of any and every opposition that can be brought to bear against us. And when the British War Council in London came to the conclusion that we must evacuate Gallipoli for strategic reasons, we left it in our own way and at our own time. Our evacuation was not a tactical reverse. We had never lost a gun or a trench during the whole of the campaign. We had never once attacked without gaining something somewhere. The evacuation was a withdrawal, a retreat even, if you like, but an exploit as creditable to our arms as most victories have been, and in some ways more surprising in its brilliant success than even our landing and occupancy. These are military facts. At the same time I am fully conscious of the sentimental side of the question, and that many of the 29th Division were glad Sir Ian Hamilton, personally, was saved the pain of yielding ground where he believed he could make it good. But in any case our landing at Gallipoli, our staying at Gallipoli while we chose, made history; may I not even say that they made British history greater? So wonderful was the sight of what our men did, and of what they endured, that we who saw must always a little pity those who were not there and could not see. We landed. We stayed. We did what the Germans had said was impossible. Not only the German press and the German people clamoured it, but the German experts of military science. *It could not be done.* Precisely. But we did it.

I got in the line of their coming, and watched the stretcher cases one by one. It is a piteous spectacle, the sight of strong men, in fullest health and great fettle but an hour ago, living, but broken and prostrate, helpless, and perhaps trembling. The first of our regiment I found was one of the machine-gun section. He tried to tell me about the advance. He had been in the thick of it, and though he could scarcely control his lips, his eyes gleamed with enthusiasm, the unquenchable enthusiasm of the true soldier. He was quite cheery, but thought we had lost a good few officers and a number of men. Beyond that I would not let him go on, for he looked as if he should husband all his strength. As I turned away I almost knocked against our pioneer sergeant. He was unconscious, and looked more like death than any living man I had then seen. (I've seen several others since.) I'm glad to say that he recovered, and was afterwards on home service. The recoveries of war are even more wonderful, I think, than its carnage, its courage, or its sacrifices.

The wounded were coming down fast now, and after a few grim minutes I cleared out of the way. I didn't feel very cheery.

I started off on a voyage of discovery along the cliff that rose abruptly behind our narrow sand-strip of beach. Before I had gone far I saw coming towards me a figure that I seemed to recognise. It turned out to be Captain Lindsay, and I was as glad to see him as if we'd been foster-brothers parted for years. It is extraordinary how your heart leaps at the sight of a familiar face at the front, when things are a bit thick, and your own people scattered. It has been said that nowhere else can a man feel more desperately lonely than he can on the Euston Road, and it is a graphic putting of a grim truth. But, believe me, there are a few places you sometimes come upon even lonelier than the Euston Road. One is in the thick of crowded battle. Sometimes you find yourself at one when you are alone in some unfamiliar byway of the enemy's country. I bombarded Lindsay with questions, and he told me his news, some of it none too good. The C.O., Lieutenant-Colonel Wilson, and the senior major, Major M'Donald, were wounded. The adjutant, Captain W. D. Hepburn, had been killed, and so had the regimental sergeant-major, R.S.M. F. Bailey; and several of our subalterns were knocked out, some for the time being, others for all time. Lindsay was pretty thoroughly done up, so I took him down to a pal of mine on one of the trawlers that by luck was just at the beach then, and the skipper produced tinned salmon, biscuits galore, and rum. I had to hurry back now and get on with my job, but I left Lindsay in good hands, tucking in vigorously. Heaven knows what or when he had eaten before! He was feeding as if it had been at some remote period, and little enough at that.

I am often asked if we had enough to eat at the Dardanelles. We had. The commissariat was ample, and the arrangements were excellent.

I fancy soldiers talk (and write) afterwards about food, more than they think at the time. My own experience is that on active service you are too busy and far too absorbed to know that you are hungry until you are very hungry indeed, and that is prevented for you as often as possible. The first few days in Gallipoli our menu was limited, chiefly, to biscuits, but there was sufficient. And even biscuits alone make a very satisfactory dinner when you are hungry enough and busy enough. After our first day on the inhospitable peninsula, with the exception of a few lean patches, we had quite a variety of good food, and always enough of it, though not always time to eat. And this is more than noteworthy, more than praiseworthy, for the commissariat difficulties could not be appreciated by any one who had not actually witnessed them. It would be futile and fatuous to attempt to enumerate or describe them, either the difficulties of selection, transport, and distribution, or those of cooking and serving. Every biscuit had been brought from Great Britain, every drop of water from Egypt. Every crumb, every sup, every utensil had been loaded, unloaded, reloaded, carried and hauled, packed, unpacked, repacked, again and again. But nothing was lost, and almost nothing was wasted. We earned our dinner in Gallipoli, but we had it, and hot for the most part. There were occasions when we trod on our own dead, and, just a little less gingerly, perhaps, on dead foes, as we stumbled, bleeding and worn, to our food, but, except in the very thick of actual battle, we had it three times a day, wholesome and abundant. And we needed it. And the men *needed* their rum, and thank Providence and a sane people they had it! No better soldier was ever recruited than Corporal Rum. He *is* the best of good familiar creatures, when he's well used, and a fine fighter and a great stayer. Not once, but twenty times, in Gallipoli, when I saw the fight he put up, and the comfort he brought in the barrel on his back, I wished that a few of the weird prohibitionist individuals might have been there. I'd have bet them, guineas to gooseberries, that inside a day they'd prefer rum-and-water or a 'Johnny Walker' and soda to a tin cup of chalky, half-warm, muddy water. But perhaps it's as well that they kept their state in London and Edinburgh, their state and their easy-chairs, their cant and their salaries. I don't think they'd have been of great use at the Dardanelles. We needed *men* in that venture. But Gallipoli, I think, would have cured their morbid (that's a mild adjective selected for print) ideas on the use of alcohol.

We are said to feed our soldiers better than any other nation does. I believe, and am glad to believe, it is true, and even a little less than true; for has it not been decreed by great authority that the ox that treadeth out the corn shall not be muzzled? The field our armies tread is a hard field; the hideous harvest they tramp out saps the strength of men and of heroes, and that strength must be fed, and well fed. Tommy is a great trencherman, and well for us that he is, and that we do him so well.

On the 28th we had been on the peninsula a scant three days. It seemed but an hour. It seemed years.

The men had done wonders. And the subalterns, boys most of them, had worked like madmen and giants. Some had come fresh from public school, some from country parsonage homes, some from counting-house and office. They had played bridge and golf yesterday; several were credited with the prettiest taste in ties; one boasted that he could order as good a feed as Newnham-Davis himself; at least three knew where the stage door of the Gaiety stood; but how they worked, how they fought, how they obeyed, how they waited! The saints of their islands must have been proud of them, Andrew, David, and Patrick, and George and his Dragon; and, by Britain and the Old Flag, we were proud of them too!

The soldier boys and the men! I think every officer there, as he looks back at those never-to-be-forgotten days and nights in Gallipoli, will be glad and eager to give pride of place to the men and the youngsters. God knows I am!

Chapter 7

The C.O.'s Story

The next day (it was 29 April) I was again running stores to the beach, and having a little time to spare in the afternoon, I went up to the hospital tents. They always seem to call one. I came across one of my own men, who told me that the C.O. was in a small bell-tent close by, and I immediately found it and him. He was lying on a stretcher, looking rather limp and very much bandaged, but wonderfully cheery – as cheerful as I had ever seen him. Yet he had just been through hell, and had come out of it not unscathed. It seemed to ease him to talk, and to do him no harm, and I was keenly glad to listen.

First of all, he gave me half-a-dozen urgent instructions, and when I had assured him that they should be carried out scrupulously, he plunged into his story.

'The battalion,' he said, 'was in reserve at first, but was ordered to take up ammunition to the firing-line. We were soon in the firing-line – right in it – and we stayed there. We had evidently got well forward, and Sergeant Allsop (the mess sergeant) was with me when suddenly a sniper appeared behind a bush, one of those damned, dusty, prickly, Eastern things, not a dozen yards, away. I wasn't quick enough, but he was. His first bullet smashed the bolt of my rifle.' [The reader may think it strange that a commanding officer should be carrying a rifle, but all officers in the early days carried rifles and were dressed like the men, except that cloth rank-badges were on their shoulders.] 'His second one got Sergeant Allsop through the stomach, and his third got me through the arm. I fancy I must have slightly wounded him, for he went off. Poor Sergeant Allsop was moaning badly, and I got my pack off somehow or other (though my pinked arm had begun to hurt damnably), and made him as comfortable as I could – it wasn't very, I know. I thought he was unconscious, but I left him my water-bottle, on the chance that it would come in handy to him later. It was practically dark by this time, and I started to make for the sea, or what I thought was the direction of the sea. The close fighting was done for that day, and I was less than no use where I was. I pushed along as best I could, into holes, over fallen men, through scrub and dirt. Presently I came to a road, and turning into it, came slap-bang on a bunch of wounded Turks sitting on the bank at the side. I suspect they were well peppered, for they made no attempt to take me prisoner, or anything else, and they were four or five to one, and your Turk's no poltroon. He's got into bad company this war, and that's about all that's the matter with him. I hauled up and had a look at them. They looked back. Then I began a parley. "Where sea?" I said to one of them. "Officer! Backsheesh! Christian?" he demanded. "Yes," I told him. He smiled. "Christian, no backsheesh, no tell." He wouldn't help me or take my bribe. And he *might* have taken the money and sent me in the wrong direction. By Jove! yes, I like the Turk.

'Well, I went on. I thought I was going right, and in about ten minutes I walked myself almost into a Turkish patrol, who promptly started to head me off. I turned and ran like blazes; haven't run so for years – not since I was at school. Fortunately I fell flop into a hole deep enough to hide me. I ricked my ankle, I think, but that was all right, for when I'd pulled about a bushel of scrub and brushwood over me I was covered up well. The Turks had a bit of a hunt. I heard them walking about, and one chap pushed a stick or something inside my camouflage and just grazed the tip of my nose. But that was quite all right too, for they didn't locate me, and in that nice, uncomfortable hole I spent the night. In the morning I was so stiff I could hardly stand up to pull myself out. But necessity's a fine lubricant, the very finest, and I did crawl out. I crawled out with great caution, and then I had a look round. I didn't do that rashly either. I made no needless display over anything, no attempt to cut a dash – not a bit. There seemed to be no one about. I could see where to go now, and I went, as quickly and as quietly and as unobtrusively as I could. I had been going straight for the enemy the evening before – good job for me I didn't reach my destination!

'Well, I was hoofing along, feeling a bit faint and done up, when, "whizz", a bullet flew past. Another "whizz", nearer this time. The next one seemed close to my head, so I flopped down as nearly as I could the way they do it at Drury Lane, and turned over on my back and pretended to be dead. I've always heard that a sniper does not come up to view his bag. Certainly this one did not, if he saw me. I lay there just about four hours. By that time I was desperate, and my legs both went to sleep (you can bet I didn't), and said – talked in their sleep, you know – that if they didn't walk soon, they would never again be able to walk at all. So we walked. But I hadn't gone twenty yards when I saw a figure that looked beautifully like a Tommy. The figure saw me at the same moment, and up went his rifle. So down I flopped again, and managed to raise my hand and wave my handkerchief. The figure came and had a look at me. To my great joy, it was one of the Essex, our old shipmates. I don't remember much more till I found myself on the beach here and in good hands.'

That ended the C.O.'s story, but not his talk. He had thought of twenty more directions to give me, and then I had to get a man to take down a lot of notes. I believe the C.O. dictated for half-an-hour. He wasn't a pretty object to look at, and you saw at a glance that he 'd been through brimstone and the heat, but his cheer and his vitality were extraordinary.

While our commander was still dictating Captain Lindsay came in, and we three had a good old regimental pow-wow. But when we thought the C.O. really ought to talk no more, Lindsay and I said, 'Cheer-o, sir,' and 'See you later, sir.' I walked a little way back with Lindsay along the cliff, and then, as I had to get back to my own 'odd jobs', I said how much I hoped to be beside him in a day or two, and we exchanged a careless, friendly good-night. He went off, whistling 'Annie Laurie'. I never saw him again. I walked back to my job. He walked on to his death.

Chapter 8

Rough-and-Ready Diplomacy

Coming back to the beach, after having parted from Lindsay, I met my pal the skipper, who, at my request, had regaled him on salmon and rum the night before. He was exulting over a Turkish rifle he carried, which he said he had begged from an ordnance officer, that it might hang, a trophy and an inspiration, in the wardroom of H.M.S. —.

'You're a lovely liar,' I told him. 'I know the wardroom it is going to decorate – somewhere in Brixton.' He solemnly winked and went on. He was a great fellow. When war was declared he was first officer on one of the big transport liners, but immediately volunteered to go anywhere and do anything, and the nearer the firing-line the better.

A little farther on I ran across Colonel Patterson, an old Guardsman who had equipped, at his own expense, a corps of Zionist Jews from Palestine, to carry water. They did excellent and merciful work all through the campaign, and one or two got mentioned. The colonel gave me a whisky, I remember. A very sensible chap; didn't believe in water only. Nor do I.

Some captious reader may wonder what my works-party was doing all this time. Oh, that was all right! I had left it in charge of a very efficient subaltern. I always believe making other people work, if possible. It does them good. And it does me good. I got down to my little lot just in time to catch our small boat, and off we went to our ship.

The next three days we were still unloading, and every one of us worked as we had never worked before. On Saturday I reported to the flagship that my party would be ready to be taken off on Sunday morning, and got a reply that this would be done at eight o'clock.

At ten o'clock on Saturday night a midshipman came on board to see the master. I have seen a good many weary men and boys since I last saw the moon rise over Melrose, but I believe that little middy was the most exhausted creature I've seen yet. He went on through sheer pluck, but his body was 'done'. I think he could have slept at the mouth of a Turkish cannon. I gave him food, for he was hungry and thirsty; but even so, I had to keep talking to him, as, if I stopped but an instant, his yellow head went on to his plate and he was fast asleep. He had been at it, without rest, since early on the 25th. It was the 31st now. War is no respecter of children.

When I had seen the midshipman off, the cabin-boy told me that the master wanted to see me. I went to his cabin, and, to my utter surprise, he said that he had orders to sail for Mudros at daybreak.

'But what about my little lot, skipper? I don't get off till eight,' I exclaimed.

'Don't know anything about you,' was the disconcerting reply. 'Orders are orders, and I sail at daybreak.'

'Now, look here, skipper,' I cried hotly – I was desperate – 'chuck your damned official tone and talk sense. I am not going with you.'

'Well, get off my boat.'

'How the devil can I get off your boat?'

'I don't know. Jump off.'

Here was a kettle of fish! I had orders to rejoin my battalion, and somehow or other I was going to rejoin. I thought hard.

Then I said, 'Look here, old man,' (I was on the tactful lay now) 'will you lend me a boat, and I'll go right to G.H.Q. by boat? Where it is I don't know, but I'll have a thorough good try to find it.'

'Oh, all right,' the master conceded; 'you can have a boat. But mind you're back by daybreak, or off I go, and your blooming Tommies 'll go with me for all I can see.'

That was a pretty prospect too! However, assuming a cheer I had not, I said gaily, 'Right-o, old man,' and rushed off and about to gather up my good old crew, by no manner of means forgetting my marine.

It was particularly quick work, but we did it. We didn't stop to parade or to polish up much brass. We didn't even stand upon the order of our going. We just went for all we were worth, every man-jack Tommy of us. Off we started, and after getting more bad language than you'd hear in a lifetime in decent Scotland flung at me by skippers of a few trawlers and other boats that we appeared likely to ram or capsize – skippers who in turn took great pleasure in trying to swamp me or cut my (borrowed) gig in two; after going in twenty wrong directions and taking twice-twenty wrong turns, and kicking up more dust generally than is usually found on the nice clean sea, we arrived at General Headquarters.

I left my crew to ship oars, or dress ship, or dance up and down on the bubbly deep, as they saw fit, and scrambled up the gangway. At its top a stalwart sentry demanded my business. 'Sentry go' is Tommy's one opportunity to treat his officer with hauteur. He rarely neglects it.

I had no idea whom to ask for, so I demanded to see Lieutenant Maule, one of our own subalterns, who was in charge of our detail of the escort of G.H.Q. I gave him a quick precis of my dilemma. Maule whistled, and then took me down to a naval officer who seemed to be a secretary. He was surrounded by pens and ink, and was flanked on every side by official books. I informed him who I was, repeated in more detail the story I had told Maule, and begged that I might be taken off before the ship sailed, instead of, as now planned, several hours after she sailed.

I was listened to, and then I was asked to take a seat and wait.

I waited. I had to. That was the reason I did – the only reason. It seemed an unconscionable while, but really before long a staff officer came in. For the third time of asking I repeated my tale. The staff officer listened, again without comment, and then he beckoned. I followed him up and down sundry stairs, through various corridors. He paused at a cabin door and told me to 'go in'. I did, and discovered a famous general at ease in his bunk, in the most beautiful pair of pyjamas I had ever seen.

For the fourth time I told my story. I was rather in a funk by this time, but that general was a brick (they usually are), and soon put me at my ease. He was amused, but he was not unsympathetic. After all, a general isn't usually very fierce in his bed and pyjamas; at least, one would imagine not. And I dare say I looked by this time as if I well might weep were I spoken to too harshly.

He told the staff officer to rout out A.P.N.T.O. (pronounced 'apinto') from his bed, and tell him to take immediate action, as every man was needed in the peninsula, and none could be spared to cruise about Mudros Bay. I was escorted back to the secretarial-looking office, and the staff officer went to get the Assistant Principal Naval Transport Officer – 'apinto'. See?

It was now the wee, sma' hours of the morning, and I was getting a bit fed-up. It looked like no bed for me that night – which the proper spirit might think quite a good joke – and I began to have visions of the good ship '*Tramp*' and her adamant skipper steaming away with my men, leaving me and my crew stranded on the G.H.Q. boat, and to see any joke in that required a broader sense of humour than mine.

Just as I was reaching that tired point when overtaxed anxiety dwindles into weak 'don't care', a gentleman appeared in a dressing-gown and spectacles. It was quite a smart dressing-gown, but dull and uninteresting after the general's pyjamas. I suspect the new arrival had a few other things on beside the two I have catalogued, but that was all I could see. He asked a little drowsily what all my story was about. I kept my temper (I jolly well had to!) and for the fifth time told my plight from the curt Alpha of the skipper's ultimatum to the horrible Omega of my unit about to be shipped back to Mudros, or some other unknown and more remote place – and they all captainless, poor things! I flatter myself I pitched the tale rather well this time. I was getting easy in my lines, and even threw in a gesture or two. I am thinking of doing it as an after-the-war recitation at At Homes and garden fêtes.

The staff officer sauntered in while I was reciting to gown and specs, and kindly chipped in most effectively. He knew it almost as well as I did by this time – and so he ought; he'd heard it often enough – and he had a larger flow of phrases; and then, too, he had had the general's orders.

Well, I did my best. But at first I thought it was all up with me. Persons hauled out of their beds are not as a rule uncommonly tractable, and the one in question looked glum. But after a bit of an argument Apinto decided to write me an order to the master of my ship to delay his sailing until an hour or so after sunrise, that I might be able to get myself and my men off, and up to Gallipoli, where we were wanted.

I have a strong suspicion that H.M. Navy wished to grab my men (unquestionably the pick of our contemptible little army) for a ship's working-party. But I have never been able to prove it, and at the time

I did not mention it. I pocketed my precious document, thanked everybody, especially that trump of a staff officer, and bolted for my row-boat.

My crew had been waiting the whole time, tossing about in the little gig. I thought then that they deserved to be 'mentioned', and I think so still.

Off we went, and ultimately we got once more alongside our floating palace. I took an exquisite delight in waking the skipper and telling him the news. I hadn't enjoyed anything so much since I was four and got my first breeks. But he returned good for evil, and opened a bottle. He was a good chap, was Captain King; one of the best.

We were all glad to go. Waiting about in war-time is desperately trying, but I think every one of us was sincerely sorry to leave the S.S. *Melville* and Captain King. I often wonder whether she is still afloat. If she is, and I can find her, I intend to board her once more and wring hands all round. Our weeks on her were the most enjoyable of all our time in the East. We all said so. She was no P. and O., but a jolly cosy home, not soon to be forgotten.

Chapter 9

Linking Up With the Battalion

We landed on W beach, and I took my detachment about two hundred yards inland and ordered them to fall out, as we had to wait for a platoon of the company that was a working-party on another transport. It was due to be on the beach at eleven.

While we waited I had a 'look round', and you may be sure the men did. It was then that I had my first glimpse of the enemy, and in a form pleasing to British eyes – a batch of prisoners who arrived soon after we did. And who should be in command of their escort but Sergeant Henderson of my former company, a man I had always particularly liked! He saw me, handed over his prisoners, and then came back to have a chat with me. As far as I could gather from him, the battalion had been having a very rough time, and I was jolly glad that I was going to take a hundred and fifty men to help them. It seemed monstrous to hang about in this comparative safety and luxury while our men were in such shambles, so I had a ramble round to try to find a staff officer, and get permission to push on. I ran one to earth before long, Major O'Hara, and he accommodatingly told me to join my battalion as soon as possible. Splendid! But where was the battalion? No one seemed to know very exactly. The sergeant was useful for general directions; for explicit ones he was useless.

Well, it was for me to find the battalion, and I had a Scots tongue in my head.

At two o'clock I formed up my company, and off we went in column of route, I marching at their head, feeling considerably pleased with myself at getting the better of H.M. Navy, the senior service, and in good spirits now that we were going to link up with our battalion and fight with it to the finish.

We marched through Sedd-el-Bahr. It had been knocked about badly. The ruin of its castle was old and picturesque, but the ugly ruin of its wretched little homes was new and raw. A huge siege-gun lay helpless on its side. It had been blown off its mounting. We passed through long matted spaces of what had been barbed wire. Those of our men who had gone before us had hacked their way through it with incredible nerve, under torturing fire. It was stronger stuff this than any I had seen before. It was German-made, I understand, and most of it German-placed. The Huns had been here before us, tutoring their Mussulman allies in all the hideous tricks of war. And a number were in the peninsula still goading, overseeing, assisting. This particular wire had a big barb every eighth of an inch, and its posts were iron, quite indestructible, and almost immovable.

Leaving Sedd-el-Bahr, we swung to the left on a rough excuse for a road. And there we began to meet a thin, sad stream of wounded French, some limping painfully on foot; others, even more to be pitied, I thought, jolting in ambulance-carts. Personally, I'd far rather have stayed lying where I fell, Turkish fire and all, than have ridden in one of those infernal springless carts over the worst road I ever saw. I call it a road, because I am at a loss for another word, but in reality it was just a twisting succession of lumps and humps, sudden rises, sudden falls, and ruts and holes everywhere.

A motor-cyclist came bumping round a corner and dashed bang into one of the carts. It fortunately was empty. He and his machine parted violently, and I went forward anxiously to see how badly he was injured. He was not hurt, and told me gaily that he did just such acrobatic tumbling every ten minutes, that he'd got rather to enjoy it, and could stand it as long as the cycle could. He righted his machine, hopped on it cheerfully, and pushed off laughing.

The heat was pretty bad, so I halted the company, left my second in command with it, and took an orderly and pushed forward to reconnoitre. I soon discovered a long line of pillars stretching away inland. They looked rather like the trees in Hobbema's 'Avenue' at first glance. But I was looking for a ruined aqueduct, and soon saw that this was it. I knew that we were on the right road, and would be, so long as we kept to the left of the pillars, and kept them in sight. I went back and ordered the 'fall in', and off we started once more. It was hot work, and we were tired and thirsty, but the thought of our battalion and the sound of the Turkish guns spurred us on. In after-weeks we grew almost deaf at times to the guns, and it was only silence that we noticed or seemed to hear. There was scarcely ever a moment's gun silence; and when there was, it was so unexpected and so startling that in very truth it assaulted our ears. But this was in the days to come; as yet the bursting voices of the guns were very eloquent to us, and we hastened on.

I came across one of our own stretcher-bearers before long, and learned from him that the battalion was about three-quarters of a mile in front of us. There was a ridge to climb a few yards farther on, and he cautioned me to do it carefully, as we'd then be under full fire.

Giving the leading platoon commander his instructions as to direction, I pushed him off in extended order over the ridge, sending on two links to keep touch. Then, after the regulation distance had been got, I sent off the second in command with No. 2 platoon. I followed with the third. My fourth platoon had already joined the regiment.

As we crested the ridge a panorama of war stretched before us. I thought I could distinguish through my glasses a regiment packed in some trenches about seven hundred yards ahead. But my observations were brief. A scream of shell just above my head was followed by dozens of others, and leaving the other regiment to its trenches, I sent a runner to my leading platoon with orders to halt and lie down, and with word to the others to follow suit. Of course, we were not going to retire, so I left my second in command to shepherd my flock, and slipped off myself, with an orderly, as it didn't seem that the Turks had much chance of hitting two lonely beings on a decent-sized plain.

To my delight, I saw two khaki-clad figures, and I made for them, feeling very proud and valiant. They turned out to be Captain M'Lagan, who was at present commanding, and the brigade major.

'What the devil do you mean by coming up like an attack?' was the disconcerting greeting that welcomed me. 'Don't you see the Turks think we are going to attack?'

And I had been so proud of myself! *Sic transit!* 'Sorry, sir,' I said humbly, 'but I came up as I had been taught.'

Captain M'Lagan grunted. 'Well, go and take your company back behind the ridge to the left, where you will find some dug-outs, and stay there for further orders.' Then he relented, and added, 'Oh, well, as you're here, send the message, and stay a bit yourself. So the orderly was banished, and not I. I was having quite a nice time watching and chatting, when a warning shout was heard: 'Lie down !' Flop I went. Scream! Bang! Bang! Dust—much dust! I thought my head was off, and turned it gingerly to have a look for my body. To my intense surprise, my body was still quite near—still fastened on, in fact.

The shell had burst about fifteen yards farther on, and there a poor machine-gunner lay clasping his gun's nozzle close in his arms (as if it were a living thing he loved), and with half his head blown away. Another gunner lay beside him, very, very still. I have often thought since that death is never quite so still anywhere else, never so completely motionless, as it is on a battlefield, or in one of the byways of active war. I suppose it is the contrast with the noise and the confusion and the demented rush and wrangle that makes the still figure seem so much more still than other dead.

I jumped up, and I thought it a narrow squeak when an object rather like a cricket-ball bounded close past my legs. I had had enough for the moment, and I hied me into a sort of redoubt conveniently near, landing myself again almost in the arms of the O.C. and the brigade major.

Again I was admonished. 'For Heaven's sake, go and get your company out of the road, or this will go on all day!' I was off like a shot. I didn't particularly care for where I was, anyway. And I belonged with my men. I reached them just as the first platoon was disappearing over the ridge, down to comparative obscurity and safety. The enemy stopped shelling after that. They had been at it furiously for some time; and the extraordinary part of it was that only two men of mine had been hit, and trifling wounds at that – an eighth of an inch off a little finger, a slight graze on an arm.

I found the trenches easily enough, distributed the company, and in a few minutes rations were opened and a meal began.

The men ate. Then they smoked. Then a few yarned and whistled and sang. Most of them took a nap.

I had a meal too, and it warmed my tired nerves like good wine, or a fire on a winter's night.

I have been asked at home if I was frightened at the front. Sometimes I was, I suppose, but I don't think I knew it. And it's my belief, as it was my observation, that very few men on active service grow 'frightened'. Really it is all too tremendous for fear. Fear is a pallid sort of thing.

War is red – very red. And men 'see red' more often than they feel fear. Jumpy you must and do feel sometimes, when you are waiting – jumpy and a bit nervy. Often hearts thump, do what you will, just as you start to go over the top. But on the top, and over it, you and fear have known the last of each other. At least, that's how I believe it is. But you don't always quite like it – not all of it.

And, if I've praised rum, now let me praise beef. There is nothing else that puts courage – British courage, not Dutch – into a tired soldier, with nerves just a bit on edge, as food does – hot food, and enough of it. You may be too keen on your job to think much of your meals, too busy to realise that you are hungry, but, by Jove! the good beef-stew makes a new man of you, and an incomparably better soldier. 'Majors it makes generals, and meaner creatures majors.' Shakespeare said that, didn't he? If he didn't, he ought to have done so.

I fed, and then I took a look round. I discovered a battery on my left so jolly well concealed that I almost did not discover it. We may not be a subtle people, but I do believe we beat the world at camouflage. The officer in charge proved to be an old member of my regiment in our Volunteer days, and we held a small 'At Home' together then and there. War is by no means all picnic, but there's a lot of picnic in it, and some of its chance meetings are distinctly jolly.

Another battery was just leaving the position. It was fine to see them limbering up, and going off at the gallop. I don't think there's a braver sight than a battery at full speed. Their going started the Turks shelling again, but it didn't last long.

Then for the first time I heard the French .75 going it. There is nothing like the sound of artillery in full flare to buck you up, when you know it's yours, your own or your Allies'. There is a wealth of protection in the sound. You come to love it. I could have hugged that .75. And many a time afterwards I have shuddered when the guns suddenly stopped. It is the silences and not the noises of battle that are hard to endure. The sudden silence of the great guns smites you with loneliness, and gives you a desolate sort of feeling of being 'on your own' and rather impotent. The brazen voice of your own cannon tells you that they who are trying to kill you are being well punished for their impudence. There is no small thing that more distinguishes soldiers from civilians than the effect upon them of the sound of the guns. This impressed me keenly on my last leave. I spent a long day and a night in London. People shrank a bit when the barrage was loudest, and a woman cried out. But to me the noise meant safety – meant that London had let slip her dogs of war, and that they were snapping mightily at the venomous German beasts of the air. But you cannot easily convince a civilian that the greater the noise the greater the safety. Of course, the accumulated noise of prolonged active service wears out human nerves and bodies. Soldiers suffer from it in the long-run.

On going back to my company I suddenly heard a 'phit' at my feet. Well, that was war-noise of another sort, a bit too near, over-familiar, and from quite the wrong party. It dawned on me that I was attracting the attention of a sniper. The Turks were pretty snipers. I moved on briskly. I had heard a lot about the sniper, but this was my first experience of him. This beggar seemed to be just back of me, and two of them were caught a little later in a small grove behind our position. Personally I have a sneaking admiration for a sniper, especially an enemy in one's own lines. I consider him a particularly brave man. His shrift is very short if he is captured, as he has great chance of being, and he knows it.

I had been at it fairly vigorously since the witching hour of 5 a.m. the day before, and without being in bed owing to my G.H.Q. jaunt.

It was improbable that I should soon be in bed again, and I began to feel decidedly nervy; so, after detailing officer on duty and sentries, and generally tucking my company in for the night, I proceeded to seek where I might lay my heavy head, and take my first sleep in Gallipolo-land.

I found a hole in a bank, and crept into it as a tired child between its nursery sheets. It was not a particularly nice hole. It was too short. It was too narrow. As a bed it had not been well made. But I rejoiced in it, and lay down gratefully, with my pack for pillow, my Burberry for blanket. And I slept. .

I woke. Something had gone bang. And I thought that the tympanum of my ear had gone with it. I jumped up just as quickly as I could. I discovered that I had been lying close to a gun of one of our own batteries. I felt greatly relieved, and snuggled in once more. Before I could fall asleep again – you may believe that it would not have taken me long if I had had the chance – 'phit-fizz-phit' something went on the ground beside me. I lay still and debated whether a bullet could hit me where I lay. I decided that it could not, and I turned over and went to sleep at once, with an infernal rattle of musketry now going on in front. 'Things seem lively' was my last thought, but I supposed I'd get a message if supports were needed. I had been told to wait for orders. And I thought the war might go on without me for this one night at any rate; so I resolved to let the war try.

I could not stay awake. I was 'done'. But even as I drifted into exhausted unconsciousness I registered a vow that I would have another officer sleeping beside me the next night. No, the Euston Road is not the most lonesome place on earth!

One advantage of sleeping in your clothes is that in the morning you need only shake yourself like a dog, and you are ready for action. But the charm even of this advantage begins to pall after a time. It was eight days after this before I got even my boots off, and then it was only for half-an-hour to wash my angry, aching feet in a muddy pea-soup of a stream.

I woke early after my first night lying 'along the battery's side, beneath the smoking cannon', and got up as I woke. My earth-hole bed had been a godsend the night before; but now, when rest and sleep had cured my fatigue, it was no couch calculated to seduce one to linger in it. It was too trap-like, too lumpy, and much too abbreviated.

We had had no casualties while I slept – the best news an officer responsible for his men can hear on waking.

Breakfast was served early. That is field etiquette. It consisted of tea, small biscuits, and bully-beef. For some short time that was the menu at every meal. Monotonous? Not a bit of it! We were hungry. True hunger knows no monotony in decent food, and ours was very decent. And soon, long before we felt aggrieved at the commissariat sameness, all sorts of dainties danced into our bill of fare: bacon; white bread, sweet and hot from the oven; fresh meat, perfectly cooked, crisp and juicy; mountains of jam – red jam, pink jam, yellow jam, green jam, purple jam, variegated jam, black jam – jam, jam, jam.

I have only once seen nerves get the better or a man. As I went along the company on that first morning I saw a chap lying on the ground. He was moaning and whimpering, and seemed to be partly comatose. I asked if he was hit, but no one seemed to know, or to know what was wrong with him. I lugged him up on to his feet, but he just fell down again. I hoisted him up again. He lay down. As fast as I pulled him up, he threw himself or fell back on to the ground. I tried to walk him up and down. I might as well have invited Achi Baba to come and waltz with me. He would lie down and groan and weep, and he would do no other thing. I tried to buck him up, to cheer him to sanity, to goad him to courage. It was no good. So I sent him off to the doctor, who told me, when I asked that afternoon, that the poor fellow was off his head, and probably would not recover.

Temperament is a queer thing, inscrutable, incalculable often. The biggest blackguard is often the finest fighter. It is curious to wonder how many corporals' canes, if not marshals' batons, are locked up and wasted at Portland and Dartmoor. The nicest men are sometimes the least reliable 'at the cannon's mouth'. And a highly strung, nervous man, who still keeps his nerve and fights well, is more to be admired – many times more – than is the apparently better and cooler soldier, a man of a lower class imbued with a kind of brutal instinct, and drugged with native dullness. The man who hates to fight, but fights, is in every way superior to the stronger hitter who likes to kill and to see blood run, and there are many of the former type in every army.

Of all the multiple pathos of war, nothing else is so terribly sad as are the little tragedies of cowardice, timidity engrained, inherited, apparent cowardice, temporary cowardice. Often only a physician, and a very great physician at that, can tell when the attack of fear – it comes in all forces now and then – is craven, mongrel fright, and when sheer, distraught illness. We see the poor wretches tremble, and run or throw themselves into any cover, or into none –

But one point must still be greatly dark:
    The moving why they do it;

and to be able to 'mark how much perchance they rue it' would be to have an omniscience not given to mortals. The heart-break and the shame that follow such breakdowns are, I believe, the most poignant and the most lasting that ever come to masculinity, the most biting remorse of which any man is capable. And yet many men do things less manly, less forgivable.

Chapter 10

The Burying-Party

Half-an-hour later, in obedience to a message, I reported for orders at Brigade Headquarters, about three hundred yards to our left front. I took an orderly with me, and was attended by a sniper. It was very annoying to be fired at without replying. That tries your nerves and your temper, if you like. I had no time to hunt snipers now, so I consigned my attentive friend to perdition, and went about my business.

At headquarters I was introduced to the general, who said my regiment had done awfully well, and that, if my lot were as good as the others, we'd be a decided acquisition. I replied that they would do their best.

Then the staff captain got hold of me, and very tactfully told me that I was going to be given an honourable but not very pleasant job, which would break the men in wonderfully. And it did.

The honourable task was burying the dead. I went back at once, of course, called the officers and non-coms together, broke the grim bit of news to them, reminded them how all-important it was to take identity-discs and papers off the bodies before burying them, and we got to work. Our C.O. shared Napoleon's theory that a general might be excused for losing a battle, but never for losing a moment; and so with any other soldier. Certainly 'Do it now' is a good rule for almost everything soldiers have to do, and for none is it a better rule than for burying-parties.

It was not pleasant work, but, in small things at least, war makes philosophers of us all. I have always had an unconquerable dislike of looking at a dead body 'laid out' at home. But on active service Providence, or whatever you like to call it, seems to step in and drug you. You grow callous. One is not indifferent, but one does not think overmuch of the solemnity. I do not say that your finer senses are really blunted (privately, I suspect that fine senses are unbluntable), but you are given a job to do, and, no matter what it is, you just do it, as being all in the day's work.

There were many of our own dead. There were more than twice as many of the Turks.

There had been a splendid bayonet-charge the night before, the action which made the battalion's name, and for it the regiment was given the post of honour for the next three days. It is almost incredible how soldiers value such rewards.

The situation had been saved by the quick order of Captain M'Lagan, the acting C.O., but the inevitable toll of war was heavy. Both the leading companies lost their commanders, Captains Lindsay and Russell; and Lieutenant Smith, the acting adjutant, was also killed. They could ill be spared; but their grit and initiative had admittedly saved an appallingly desperate situation, and for it their regiment was mentioned in despatches. They laid down their lives blithely enough, I was told; and this it was easy to believe. They died to save others as truly and simply as ever was done, and I am sure they died where they would, could they have chosen – at the head of their men. I left my second in command to bury them, and went off to see how the party burying the enemy was doing it. I had split our burying-party into two – one to look to our own dead, one to deal with the Turks. I had no doubt that the two parties would handle the bodies of foe and of friend alike, but it seemed more decent, as well as distinctly my job, to *see* for myself. Well, I saw.

A burn ran down the centre of our position, just such a mossy, bubbly, friendly thing as I had waded in and fished in a thousand times in Scotland. It was full of dead Turks. We had to wade in and pull them out. Most of them were heavy. All of them were sodden and water-logged. Water and slime oozed and squelched from their clothes as we hauled them about. It was a tough and a dirty job, but it was done as decently as it could be.

The side of the bank of the nullah was quite ten feet high, and crouched against it were seven Turks. Two were smiling broadly – and all were stone-dead. Three of them were leaning up against three others, and the seventh was keeping them all up, propping and holding them. He had crept in among them, his face to the cliff, and all you could see of him was his back and his heels. Seven Turks as dead as dead could be, and only one of the seven had a mark! His mark was ugly enough, for seventy. The top of his head had been blown off exactly as you crack off the top of an egg. About fifteen yards away was the body of another Turk, disembowelled. He was an appalling sight. Evidently one of our awful 'Lizzie' shells had dropped there, and its concussion alone had killed six of the enemy. I had heard a great deal of soldiers being killed by concussion. This was the first time I saw it.

The Turk wears an extraordinary amount of clothing, especially round his middle, which is encircled by never-ending yards and yards of cloth. He must be a great believer in keeping his stomach warm. And, in hot countries, no idea could be sounder. Would that we could succeed in drumming it into Tommy. In Gallipoli a great number of our men persisted in taking off their body-bands against orders, and invariably these were the first to contract dysentery. They got hot during the day, and in the chill of the evening naturally started to shiver. Then the trouble began. And nine times out of ten the body-band would have proved a preventive. Tommy is a lovable creature, but he is not always tractable, and often he is not teachable.

We buried sixty-two Turks that day, and most of them were *Nizam* troops, highly trained Regulars. They were all tall and well built. The majority of them were handsome fellows. Instead of the identity-disc our men wear, the Turk wears a small three-cornered leather bag slung from his neck. There is a paper in it with evidently a lot of information, but whether extracts from the Koran or personal details or what I was unable to tell. I could not read it.

I saw my first dead German officer on that occasion. Really they did do themselves well. He had a fine Mauser pistol with a stock that you could make into a butt and use from the shoulder, up to twelve hundred yards, I think. His binoculars were splendid – the best I ever looked through.

Towards the end of my long rounds I came to a party that was burying some of our own men, and among the dead there lay the piper, his arm about his bag, his cheek on his pipes. It is often said that the bandsmen do not take their instruments into action; and I rather think it is in regulations that they should not. But we had with us in Gallipoli more than one piper who went into action, his pipes with him. In the old days the band acted as stretcher-bearers. Music is an enormous asset at the front. More might wisely be done with it, I hold. And I believe that it might with the greatest advantage be employed nearer the fighting-line than it commonly is. Of course, the difficulties of transport and of thoroughfare, already enormous in any serious campaign, grow tremendously greater the nearer the firing-front one gets; mobility is an acute desideratum, and every commander is desperately anxious to hamper and burden his troops as little as possible. But no general would order arms or munitions to be thrown away for the sake of enabling the men to travel light when they dash at the enemy, and there are times when troops find a reasonable amount of music – even under fire – a valuable aid to bayonet and gun. And in the safer phases of war the usefulness of the band and of the impromptu amateur singsong is very great. Often in Gallipoli at night we heard the men singing, songs for the most part we had frequently heard at home, some of them songs we had heard in our cradles. Doubtless you do not remember what songs you heard in your youngest days, but equally of course those same songs make a very special appeal to you always, and nowhere, I believe, more than in soldiers' exile. I think it invariably both pleased and stiffened us to hear the men singing in the instance. I know it always meant something to me and did something to me to hear the Pipes at the Dardanelles. They seemed even more Celtic than they had done in Scotland.

I had liked the piper we had buried for himself, and I had liked him for his music. They had been good pipes, his pipes. But I was not sorry that they had gone with him into the roll of honour. It seemed fitter so. They seemed very still; but perhaps their spirit followed his, whispering in soft, ghostly numbers 'The Flowers of the Forest'.

What this piper had been through at the last I could not guess. He was badly battered, and his pipes were smashed as badly as he was. But he had stuck to them through it all, and that was soldierly of him, I thought, for surely they were his chief weapon. Puir laddie! far awa' frae hame, we buried him gently, and we laid his pipes on his grave. I passed by it three weeks later, and they were still there, sentinelling his dust, and marking his grave as no stone could have done. They told his story very eloquently, I thought, he and they muted in youth, broken in exile.

We laid six of our boys side by side in one grave, and I took out my prayer-book and read part of the burial service, before we turned and left them to keep their long state in Gallipoli. As we went one of the men came up to me with tears running down his face, and said in an odd voice, 'Oh sir, I never thought much about it till you started to read those prayers, and then, somehow, it seemed quite different.' He had always been a dare-devil of a chap, and sometimes incorrigible.

It was a beautiful day. I think it was the most intensely blue of all the vivid blue days I saw at Gallipoli. The air danced and shimmered as if full of infinitely small dust of blue diamonds. Butterflies swam through as if a thousand wild-flowers perfumed it. Always there in the radiant days of the brief early summer our eyes saw great patches of bloom, except where they beheld only desolation, aridity, death, and blood. Achi Baba, ever the most prominent mark in the view, loomed like a lump of awkwardness in the near distance, so shapeless that its very ugliness was picturesque. The sun went down in glory and in rainbows of fire as we worked, and the guns a little farther inland – the never-ceasing guns – belched out a venomous requiem and a reiterated threat.

And so – we buried our dead.

Chapter 11

The Saddest 'Bit' of All

I had to go carefully through all the papers and other belongings that had been taken off the bodies. I think that was about the saddest task; certainly it was the hardest thing I did in the Dardanelles. I seemed to be taking a beastly liberty with the dead, and at the same time with their living kindred too!

Writing home to the relatives you did not know was trying work. It was impossible to say something fresh and different to each, and it was loathsome to repeat the same forms of regret and appreciation until they became stereotyped, and to you, at least, appeared cold and artificial. The men had all done so splendidly. And there was so little to say! There was nothing worth saying that could be said. 'The War Office regrets' is formal and perfunctory, Heaven knows, but I rather think it is the kindest of all.

But I at least found even harder than writing to the men's people the scrutinising and handling of their poor little belongings. They had treasured the oddest things often, and very often the most commonplace. And the odder the thing the dead man had cherished, or the more commonplace, the more uncomfortable I felt, the more intensely guilty of desecration. The contents of some of their pockets were enough to make a fellow-corpse laugh, and again and again they were very nearly enough to make one living fellow-Scot weep.

The man we had thought the biggest blackguard and the most hardened in the regiment, had carried a baby's curl folded away in a tattered bit of silver paper. A private I had put down as ignorant and common, judging him I scarcely know from what – for I do not remember having heard him speak – had on him an unfinished letter of his own. It was especially well written, Greek e's, scrupulous punctuation, and its diction was almost distinguished. There were love-letters that had come from Scotland, and two that would go there unfinished. An old-fashioned prayer, written out in a cramped, ignorant hand, was signed 'Mother', and wrapped about three battered 'fags'. A child's first letter to 'Daddy', printed, crooked, ill-spelt, looked as if it had been carried for years. Scraps of newspapers – one containing a poem, one the report of a prize-fight – a knot of blue ribbon, a small magnifying-glass, a pack of cards, a mouth-organ (of course), three exquisite butterflies carefully pressed in an old pocket-book, a woman's ring, a snow-white curl, a race handkerchief, a paper of peppermints, and a score of still stranger things, which I will not catalogue lest any might by odd chance be recognised, and give pain – these were some of the mementoes I had to sort, and, if possible, send back to the owner's home. Almost every pocket had a photograph; most of them had several. In a dozen pockets I found the pictured face of an old woman, a severe, indomitable old woman – if her picture reported her aright – but with tender eyes; unmistakably Scots, unmistakably 'Mother'.

'Knit two and purl one;
  Stir the fire and knit again.
  And, oh, my son, my only son,
  I think of you in wind and rain,
  In rain and wind, 'neath fire and shell,
  Going along the road to hell

On earth, in wind and rain.
My little son, my only son, …
Knit two and purl one;
Stir the fire and knit again.'

It was desperate work. It choked me, and I don't mind who knows it. But one thing it established in my mind for all time: Tommy 'has his feelings'.

There were pictures of sweethearts (they said so on the back), pictures of wives, and pictures of kiddies dressed in their best. But what touched me most, and gave me a new and nobler view of Tommy, were the pictures of 'Mother'.

But my saddest find of all was a pocket in which there was – nothing! Had he lived quite alone? Had no one cared? Had he not even a memory to treasure in some poor tangible token? Had he been all his life as he died – quite, quite alone?

The letters these dead men had cherished were pitiful reading; and many of them had to be read in hope of a clue as to what had better be done with them. It would not always be kind to send everything in dead Tommy's pockets to his wife or his mother, or even to his maiden aunt.

They were pitiful reading because they said so little, and yet the men had clung to them. Often every letter in one pocket was, but for its date, identical with all the other letters. In one poor fellow's wallet were three letters, less than a page each, and without even a differing date to distinguish one from the other. They were undated, and might have been written and posted on the same day, had not their postmarks denied it. They gave no address, were alike word for word, and signed merely 'Nan'. To quote them would be brutal, not because of what they said, but because they said nothing. Yet they had been kept, and their keeper had gone to his death as a soldier.

The man at the front is hungry for home news. Can his woman think of nothing to say to him? Of course she can. But she does not know how to say it. Letter-writing is the last of the arts to be picked up, and it has not been taught as it should have been at our schools. So Tommy abroad has to read between the dumb, ill-written lines of her letters. To do him justice, he seems to do it, too, wonderfully. And to do her justice, his own letters are usually as wordless and vacant. Take this from me, for I have looked over his shoulder, and know: censoring men's letters is dull work; it is not difficult or exacting. He was born to fight and to die, our average private, and he does both about as well as they can be done. But he is very infrequently a born or a brilliant war-correspondent. There is a newspaper proprietor in London who can, it is said, make in six months an admirable editor out of any unlettered office-boy. Not all the millionaires with executive genius that own from Printing House Square to Kingsway could in a hundred years make an Archie Forbes out of Tommy.

I found a small dictionary in one man's tunic, *Sartor Resartus* in another, in a third a Murray's time-table. Several had carried a Testament, and two of the Roman Catholics had their beads.

Chapter 12

The Battle of Fir-Tree Wood – The First Phase

The next two days were spent in settling down to the pick, pick, pick of trench warfare, and to the holding of positions already won. By now my men had all been under fire, and they were as jolly as possible, although we had a casualty every little while, and each of us knew that it might be his turn next. But it takes a thundering lot to depress Mr Thomas Atkins, and to stop him from seeing some humour even in the most critical situation. If there is anything ridiculous to see, he sees it and chuckles at it, though he has to see it through blood, to chuckle between death-groans. If there is nothing ridiculous, he invents it. His laugh he must and will have. And I have no doubt that it is this indestructible quality of bubbling jollity that keeps our men the most contented and the most manageable of all armies.

In Gallipoli the so-called 'rest-camp' or reserve-trench was the most dangerous place. In the firing-line, so long as you kept your head well down, was really the safest place, except just when you were going over the top; that was hot always. In the support trenches you usually got shelled, and the snipers paid you their best attention. The shells and the bullets that went over the top of the firing-line (as more did than didn't) found their way to the reserve trenches. And you were always under fire in every part of the damned peninsula. There was no real cover. In the firing-line you got some of the shots intended for you; out of it you got all the shots intended for you, and a great many that were not.

I remember a small shell landing in the cook's fire and scattering it all over the place. Nobody was hurt, but the cook's feelings were. Most cooks are irascible, and to this rule army cooks are no exception. Another time I happened to be standing near three or four men who were watching a mess tin, full of tea, boiling on a small fire of their own. The owner of the tin went away for a moment, when 'whack' went a bullet straight through the precious utensil. Curiously enough, it did not topple over, but it began to leak badly. The men screamed with laughter, and the owner hurried back. He was furious with his fellows; he thought they were playing a trick on him, and it took some time to make him believe that the practical joker was a bullet.

The snipers seemed particularly busy near our trenches in those first days, but indeed they were all over the place. We used to organise parties to hunt for them. It was like going out for a day's shooting at home, only a little more risky. For very obvious reasons, the sniper usually didn't try to pot you when he saw that you were hunting for him: first, his shooting would tell where he was, or at least the direction he was in; and, second, if he were caught, he would be uncommonly lucky to be taken alive.

I remember watching a party of the Essex having a sniper-hunt. Suddenly a man stopped under a tree, up went his rifle, and down lurched a Turk. The hunters all gave one whoop of delight and rushed to view the awful 'bag'. Tommy never seemed indifferent to the foe when he had killed him. Our Indian soldiers took no interest in an enemy after they had killed him. One of our wounded officers told me long afterwards that while he was walking to the dressing-station a Turk's head landed at his feet, having fallen from a tree just ahead. There must have been some scuffle in its leafy branches, but he had noticed nothing. A Gurkha came calmly down as he passed, wiping his knife with tender care. He saluted punctiliously, but did not even glance at his bleeding trophy in the dust, or at the something horrid that was now seen hanging, heavy and dripping, caught in two interlaced branches. The Turk is a wonderful climber – miraculous, when you consider his bolsters and blankets of clothing. The Indian climbs like a monkey, and will follow his prey anywhere, under the earth, over it, off it. I suspect Indians will be our supreme airmen before long. The native troops we had with us at the Dardanelles were all splendid soldiers. But it was whispered in the trenches that the Mussulmans among them did not altogether like taking the lives of the Mussulman Turks. Well, I hope Turkey will be on our side in the next great war – if there is one – and I think she will.

We one day caught a sniper standing on a platform he had so fixed in a hole in the ground that his head and shoulders were in a bush. He had painted his face green, and in the cache of his hole he had enough food and ammunition to last him weeks. And I say again that the sniper is a brave man. This man's ammunition and provender were excellent. We used the food.

Thirst was the greatest plague of my first days in the trenches, and the chalky water, which was all one ever came across – and that not often – made the thirst almost worse. But after the first few days thirst never troubled me much. And I used to smoke all day long. Tobacco at the front! Believe me, you do not know what the word 'solace' means unless you've had smokes at the front. Tobacco is every commander's most valuable aide-de-camp. It is the master diplomatist of every campaign. I don't know what one would do without it on active service; and I have no wish to know. A cigarette is the first thing a wounded man asks for, almost invariably. And it was tobacco more than anything else that made the trenches home to our soldiers. Tommy is a domestic animal, if ever there was one, and I have seen nothing more pathetic than his desperate contrivances and attempts at domesticity in the vermin-ridden trenches of Gallipoli and on the blood-soaked plains of Flanders. He sticks his bits of pictures up on the mud walls somehow, he has his remarkable singsongs, and he lights his pipe. Sometimes his songs are ribald, but it is oftener, I think, to cloak a sentiment and an emotion about which he is shy than it is native coarseness.

On our third day in the trenches an order came that an advance was to be carried out, and a little after noon we went up towards the battle of Fir-Tree Wood, going in two columns in file, keeping touch, and keeping well in the nullahs and in the natural folds of the ground.

We came to our positions, and learned that we were in reserve. It was not a comfortable position. It lacked repose. The enemy's machine-guns were infernally busy, and we had to lie very low, or get picked off. We lay low. The junction of two of the nullahs was just here, and it became a famous spot afterwards, being known as Clapham Junction.

I packed my company into a convenient depression, and for the moment they were fairly comfortable. I slipped across the burn running beside us to see the C.O. 'Burn' is not a slip of my Scots pen. Scotland and Gallipoli have many characteristics in common, and often the gruesome peninsula looked weirdly like 'hame'. Sometimes in the gloaming I could almost hear the pipes of home playing; and at night, in the cutting Gallipoli cold, often I thought I smelt the snow blown across the dead and withered heather.

Captain M'Lagan, acting adjutant, was beside Captain Macintosh, the senior captain and acting C.O., who had arrived from the beach two days before, and was now in a place that might be accurately described as a golf bunker. Macintosh, M'Lagan, and I chatted for a little. But there were no orders for me yet, so I left them, and ran down the brae to reconnoitre the company behind mine, just to see that we were all keeping touch, for it would soon be dark. I was talking to the company's captain when suddenly a quick, wicked whisper ran down to us through the men.

'The C.O.'s killed,' it hissed.

'Good God, no!' I cried; 'it can't be true. I was talking to him just *now*. I left him only a minute ago.'

But it was too true.

Often the despatches of war are mercifully quick.

I could have sworn that the place where he was sitting and where I had left him was as safe as Whitehall. It must have been a long-range bullet with a high trajectory that found him and pierced his head. The adjutant was sitting just below him, actually leaning against his knee, writing out an order. The C.O. stopped short in the dictation. The adjutant heard a soft sigh, looked up, and all was over.

So died 'a very gallant gentleman', respected by all who knew him, loved by all who served under him. His own company were devoted to him.

To me the saddest part was that he had been in the cursed peninsula only two days. He was one of the champion athletes of Scotland in his younger days, and it had been our ambition to see him leading his men in a bayonet-charge. Would that he had died in such a way rather than by a bullet fired at a venture!

We shall not soon forgive Gallipoli his death.

But we had scant time for grief then. Even as we caught our breath and said 'It cannot be true!', orders came for the battalion to go up to the front line to fill a gap, and off it set, a platoon at a time, in extended order, over the ridge. It was practically dark when a further order came for the remainder of the battalion to reinforce, and off we went, into the next battle of our Gallipoli campaign. For me it was my first battle anywhere.

Up the nullah we went in file, and then swung to our left. The great difficulty – and it was very great – was to keep touch, especially when a man got hit. Then instantly, click, like a stop-watch, his pals halted, gathered round him, leaving our game of war to play itself, caring nothing for the Turk (that would come later), and not too much for orders.

I had to keep barging up and down the lines, something like the distracted captain of a badly-in-hand 'footer' team. The only thing to do when a man fell was, if he lived, to pull him, as gently as we could, to the side, and leave him there, with a field dressing on (we always managed that), at the same time passing the word for stretcher-bearers. Some at home may call this callous, but it was not. It was merely war. It was our job to keep touch, and everything had to give way to it. It was better, too, more merciful even, that one life should be destroyed than twenty, and that was the proportionate cost of even brief delay.

We reached the firing-line. We found every one digging furiously. Bullets were flying everywhere, thick and fast as flakes in a northern snowstorm, and bullets whizzing about one are a wonderful stimulus to one's arm-power. No one was talking. The men scarcely looked up at us as we came. They just dug, dug, dug, like infuriated fiends. And sooner than I can tell it we were digging too.

I sometimes think that this war should go down in history as the War of Spades. Certainly the Dardanelles campaign was fought with that homely garden tool. I once heard a woman name forty-six things she could do with a hairpin. It was a poor soldier that couldn't do sixty-four with a spade after a month in Gallipoli. The spade was our father and our mother. When the hell was hottest we advanced a few paces, and then dug ourselves in. More than once the men dug until they began to fall asleep digging. One chap slid gently to earth, pillowed on his spade, and began to snore. A pal rolled him over and over down the easy incline of the half-finished trench, and there he lay, the picture of dishevelled peace, still snoring.

The British Isles should bloom like the rose after this war, for millions of gardeners are coming home from the war to England and Scotland and Ireland and Wales, the expert diggers of all the world, artists in spade-work, drilled and taught and perfected in German East Africa, in Mesopotamia, in Egypt, in Macedonia, in Palestine and France, and in our own Gallipoli.

Soon it was found that there were too many in the firing-line, and two companies were sent back to a small nullah about three hundred yards in the rear, and we were one of them.

How we all got into position I don't know. It was black dark, and we were crowded to the point of cramp. My own job was standing in the middle of an unknown field, and trying to direct a seething lot of excited men struggling about over the treacherous broken ground in the dark. Anybody could have had my job for a tin bawbee, with pleasure. The cursed nightly fusillade had begun. But I got them all over and tucked into our temporary quarters.

The little nullah we were in had a very high smell – quite the highest I ever encountered. Tommy can live without roses, and often he has to; but Tommy sniffed, and Tommy swore. 'Pass the ohder Cologne', was the mildest comment I overheard, and I heard many. We wondered what the mischief it was. But at dawn we wondered no more. Our nullah was half-full of dead Turks. They were very dead. And there was other filth there, less describable and no sweeter.

I had now taken over the duties of an adjutant. 'Adjutant' has a mighty fine sound, but be not deceived. An adjutant is a charwoman in trousers and gold lace; and there was not much gold lace at Gallipoli.

My adjutancy entailed a lot of painful wandering about, searching for things not to be found, etc, for returns have to go in to headquarters exactly as in normal times. And it's 'Adjutant' this and 'Adjutant' that, until a fellow's head whirls and twirls as if he were a dancing dervish. I hope never to hear the word after the war.

I had had nothing to eat since early the day before. There literally had not been time. But I took time now, and thoroughly enjoyed bully-beef, biscuits, and water.

Refreshed, but not feeling altogether like a lion, I started off to try to find out what was going on. I suspect I have some share of Tommy's child-like and quenchless curiosity. I know I did a world of prying about on my own account while we were at the Dardanelles, and sometimes I did it on legs so tired and feet so sore that they might perhaps have been better employed in doing nothing; but then, as I once heard a caustic sergeant-major say irascibly, 'Somebody blooming well has to take a little interest.' Well, I certainly took an interest; but, for all that, I suspect that my peregrinations were more an indulgence than the flame of a burning sense of duty. I got back from this one of my many pilgrimages just as my watch showed eight, and I found Captain M'Lagan, who was commanding now, looking for me. He showed me a pink slip which read: 'The 5th Royal Scots will take the wood at all costs, and attack at 10 a.m. – G.O.C. 29th Division.' No long screed of instructions, no barrage-table, no movement-table in those days. A clear and concise order, as laid down in the Manual. We were up against the real thing now!

I suggested to Captain M'Lagan that, as it was my job, I'd better go and make a reconnaissance. But he wouldn't have it, for an order had recently come through that senior officers were not to expose themselves unnecessarily. To be quite frank, I wasn't gasping for the job (nor were my legs and their extremities), but I knew that it ought to be done, and I thought emphatically that it ought to be done by me, and so would any one else in my place. You do not always like your job of the moment on active service, but you are always ready to do it, and to do your best. It is a remarkable thing, human nature being what it is, and service fatigue what it is, but it is absolutely true both of the professionals (Regulars) and of the amateurs (Volunteers) in the army that, whatever their job is, they always have a try at it. I have known men grow nervy, I have seen men break down, when they had done all men could do, borne all men could bear, but I have never seen a man disgrace himself by funking or hesitating to tackle his 'bit'. I suppose there are bound to have been such cases. It's uncontrollable temperamental handicap when it does happen, I fancy.

Forbidden to go myself, I called for volunteers to make a reconnaissance, and the difficulty was to pick from among the many who pushed forward. I selected five, and put in charge a man who had once been in the Foreign Legion. And I told him that he would be recommended whether he came back or not. The chances were against him, and we both knew it.

Off they went.

And they all came back! That was very remarkable. We were all greatly surprised – and so were they. The private in charge brought back an excellent report and a sketch of the enemy's position that proved invaluable. He was recommended and got the D.C.M. for that day's work. He was wounded three weeks later, and died in hospital.

The attack started. We got into the wood, and hung on till four in the afternoon. But the battalion got hell from the machine-guns. The

C.O. and I, with our orderlies, had moved up to the jumping-off place, which was the firing-line three hundred yards in front of our stench-ridden nullah. We stood it, waiting for further orders and reports, as long as our nerves would let us. But nothing came. After two hours (an hour is a long time in battle) we sent off an orderly to glean what he could. He never came back. We sent off another. He did not come back either. Then the C.O. went off himself to reconnoitre, I being left where I was to receive any reports that might come in, and to act on them.

At last a report came in from one of the captains saying they were in the wood, but could not hold on much longer, and that he was the only officer left.

The C.O. hadn't come back, and I began to feel fidgety, when suddenly he came along, looking very grave.

'They are getting knocked about on the left,' he said.

'And on the right too,' I told him, handing him the pink slip.

'Damn that!' was his comment. 'This doesn't look hopeful.'

'Damn' is more than an oath sometimes. I thought it was as sad a word as I had ever heard as it fell from the C.O.'s lips.

'No,' I agreed; 'it looks very far from hopeful. And, look here, sir, it is my turn now to reconnoitre.'

He nodded grimly. 'All right. Off you go.'

And I went, running as hard as I could and as long as I could, till I came to a tree, banged into it, and flopped down rather hard. I was half-stunned for a moment; but it quickly dawned upon me that one old tree was a silly place to halt at, so I did another bolt, and sprinted on till I landed in a nullah. Just where I landed I found another of our captains, so they were not all killed – yet. I gave him some orders and started to get back. I was running like blazes, when a pain like a red-hot iron shot through my side. Down I went, spread-eagle fashion, about five yards from a trench, and gasped out, 'I've got it at last.'

A voice that I seemed to know called from the trenches, 'What's wrong?'

I moved my head round, and saw my old second in command, Captain J. W. S. Wilson, latterly well known to all in the Mediterranean Expeditionary Force. I had scarcely seen him since we landed. He was wounded, badly smashed, but he was confoundedly cheery. I felt like overdone porridge, and had just as much spine in me.

'Oh, I've got it this time,' I insisted. 'For God's sake, get some one to take my pack off!'

In those days we fought in full marching order, but I believe it was the very next day that we stopped that, and dumped our packs before we went into the thick of it – dumped them all together under a guard when we could, for passers-by had a habit of rummaging. Every man in that army was a splendid fighter, but not all of them were strictly—— But there, I said before that Tommy is as inquisitive as a monkey.

I remember rolling over twice, and some one pulled my stuff off. All sorts of thoughts flashed through my mind. I thought of Scotland and a garden where the reddest roses in Edinburgh grow, and I thought quite a good deal of the Germans. It was odd – and yet not so very odd, perhaps – but all through Gallipoli I felt that we were fighting the Germans, and often forgot, even when killing them, that we were fighting the Turks. And I've heard a dozen officers say much the same thing. Of course, there were Hun officers thickly scattered among the Turks, and we heard their arrogant guttural voices constantly. The voice was the voice of Jacob, and often it was his hand too that we felt, his brain that we met.

I thought I was shot through the lungs, and I was rather restless, and pitched about, and tried to sit up. My old friend charged me not to get up at any cost, as the bullets were just shaving me. I had thought they were singing pretty close, and I knew the vermin bit!

The pain grew a little easier (that's the best of pain), and I suddenly began to laugh like blazes. I can hear myself yet. I tried to stop, but I could not stop. I thought I was going to keep on laughing madly for ever. 'You don't seem very bad,' some one said. 'No, you silly blighter,' I returned, while tears of idiotic merriment ran down my face; 'I'm not even hit. Do you know what it is? It's a stitch in my side. Oh! Ho! Oh!' But all the same I was in doubt as to what was causing my torment. It was infernal.

Men have died from having their eyes bandaged, and some one then drawing a bit of ice over their throats and pouring warm water down their backs. And I believe, if any one had told me that he could see blood coming from me, I should have fainted, and felt sure as I did so that it was death.

I had to lie without moving for over two hours. It was terrible. One or two shells landed perilously near. One of them hit a poor fellow already badly wounded. His cries were almost more than one could endure. But, like a great deal else in war, endure it we had to do. There is hardly anything much sadder than the stricken cry of a wounded man who cannot move hand or foot, sometimes cannot even turn his face into the shelter of the earth, or of his coat, when the shells and the bullets are landing thick about him.

However, the fire slackened sooner or later, and I got up somehow (the relief of being able to move eased my pain wonderfully), and bolted to the C.O., who had quite made up his mind that I'd been killed. He listened to me, and then made out a report. But who was to take it? We hadn't an orderly left.

A young bugler, overhearing, volunteered to go back to General Headquarters with the message. He had been carrying ammunition all day long, up hillocks, down steeps, over brooks, into nullahs, and he looked dead-beat with fatigue. But he saluted with a smile, and went off into a hell-rain of bullets, for the hail of fire had begun again, and, it seemed to us, with added fury. I watched him through my glasses. Before he had gone fifty yards he was enveloped in a cloud of dust from a bursting shell.

'My God, sir, he's down!' I cried. 'No, no; he's up and running. Good lad! Damn it all, he's down again! I'm afraid he has got it this time. I can't see any more of him.'

We could get no one else at the moment to go with a duplicate report, so we had to risk it. He might get through, or headquarters might learn in some other way what we had reported.

But the boy got through. He hobbled into headquarters dragging a shrapnel-riddled leg, and begged to come back to us with the answer. He was 'right enough; only a flesh-scratch that wouldn't keep a girl from a dance.' But the general sent him off to the dressing-station, rebellious and ungrateful. He got the D.C.M. As far as I know, he is still alive. But you lose sight of men provokingly on active service.

A report came down to us, though, to try to charge into the wood, as supports were coming up to the Turks, and all our push was needed at what threatened to become a weak spot. We got in – in a way – but we had to get back to our first front line. I went down to the right again, and I saw the Border Regiment advancing to the attack. It was magnificent. To watch them made me tingle then, and to think of it makes me tingle now, and I am very tired as I write this to-night, in another dug-out, somewhere in Flanders, and not too full of the ready electricity of enthusiasm.

I shall never forget one of the Border sergeants leading his section. He shouted to his men, just as they came to the edge of our trench, 'Come on, lads; jump over!' And over our heads they all went.

Two of them were hit, just ten yards farther on. One of them never moved again. The other lay groaning pitifully, so two of our men rushed out and brought him in.

I myself saw fifty things done that deserved mention. But it was impossible to record them all. There was always a grave chance when you recommended a man that you had overlooked something still braver that another had done, but you can't recommend everybody.

The Borderers got just to the edge of the wood, and there they were held up, and dug themselves in. It was wonderful to see how quickly and skilfully they did it; not a spadeful of earth was bungled, not a stroke wasted or misdirected. In Gallipoli you learned how to dig. 'Cook's son, duke's son,' you all learned to dig.

We heard now that the Australians were going to attack. And when they did, it was the sight of all that wonderful day. I wish I could describe something of the picture of war. It is indescribable, for me at least. But no pen, no brush, can overdraw or overcolour it. It is terrible, but superb.

Our own show was good, I know; but I was busy in that, and had no time to play spectator. I felt it, and I heard it; I even smelt it; but I did not see it – I couldn't.

But I saw the Australians. Wave after wave of men came across the ridge in splendid order. Oh, they were matchless! The enemy's shelling was shifted on to them in one great concentration of hell. The machine-guns bellowed and poured on them sheets of flame and of ragged death, buried them alive. They were disembowelled. Their clothing caught five, and their flesh hissed and cooked before the burning rags could be torn off or beaten out. But what of it? Why, nothing! They were as devils from a hell bigger and hotter. Nothing could stop them. They were at home in hell-fire, and they caressed it back when it licked and kissed them. They laughed at it; they sang through it. Their pluck was titanic. They were not men, but gods, demons infuriated. We saw them fall by the score. But what of that? Not for one breath did the great line waver or break. On and up it went, up and on, as steady and proud as if on parade. A seasoned staff officer watching choked with his own admiration. Our men tore off their helmets and waved them, and poured cheer after cheer after those wonderful Anzacs. 'Australia will be there!' 'By the living God that made us,' Australia was there!

On to the face of the guns, into the wood and through it, they went, torn, bleeding, undaunted. So cunningly were the damned spitting machine-guns concealed that the valiant fellows passed through and over and under them, and did not see them. Mix German beastliness with Turkish cunning, and you've brewed hell-broth indeed.

They seemed to have cleared the wood. They thought they had done so, and we looking on thought so too. They turned to come back, almost at ease, and then they got Hades indeed. Every hidden gun broke out, its venomous torture and death dribbling and frothing like foam from the mouths of mad dogs. What the Anzacs suffered then could not be told, but they came proudly on and through. They finished their job.

They were few when they came back to us into the open, to rest a bit in our trenches. And many a splendid Anzac lay resting and rotting in Fir-Tree Wood.

The day was done now, and night was wrapping the peninsula in 'the blanket of the dark'. The day was gone, and all we had managed to do was to get slightly forward on the left. This the Australians did manage. And on the right the Borderers had gained some ground.

We were tired. We were hungry. But the men were crammed full of grim determination. They were great, our soldiers, ready to fight to the last gasp, and tuned to fight to the death. Would to Heaven the Turk had come on that same night to counterattack! It might have hastened history. But the Turk had had enough.

The excitement of battle was over for the moment. I had had practically nothing to eat for two days, and the men had not had too much, or too much time in which to eat it. I had a few biscuits in my pocket, and I took them out and munched them. Food never tasted more delicious. The men had to start to consolidate and improve the position. There was worse to come, and we knew it. But they managed to light a few small fires before it was quite dark, so that tea could be had, to wash down the bully-beef and the biscuits. And the Turkish moon rose high over Samothrace, and ten thousand times ten stars glittered like fire-flies over Achi Baba.

Beyond one or two stand-to's during the night, nothing exciting happened, and the first phase of the battle was over.

I shall not forget it, my first day of battle. Some men forget their first love. No soldier can ever forget his first battle.

Chapter 13

The Battle of Fir-Tree Wood – Second Phase

.

T he next morning gave us a little breathing-space; and to me it gave an opportunity of getting 'the hang' of the position, and of forming an idea of our casualties. One of our best subalterns had been killed. Three subalterns and a captain were wounded.

At this period it was very difficult to get the wounded away. The stretcher-bearers had already been pretty well knocked about, and it meant two effective soldiers' lives risked, to each wounded man, in the endeavour to get them taken back. This entailed keeping the wounded till nightfall, when a few men could be spared. But this too was dangerous, for the peninsula was a most peculiar place to walk about in at night – you never knew the minute you might go head over heels into a nullah. The place abounded in nullahs, cracks, and fissures.

All art is cruel, and, though it rewards greatly, it demands and exacts great sacrifice. War is the cruellest art of all. To wage it mercifully and tenderly is to wage it ineffectually. And usually to make the attempt is futile and fatuous. To say that in these days we do too little for our wounded is to be absurd. We do our utmost for them, sometimes even to the detriment of the very cause for which they have given themselves. It might even be argued that we do too much. I am not contending that we should do less, and, when any war point is to be gained by it, sacrifice anew the sick and the maimed, who have already sacrificed themselves. But such a policy can be defended with some show of logic, and though one's gorge rises (mine does) at the suggestion, one's reason cannot so readily reject it.

It was sometimes a difficult problem to solve in Gallipoli. The stretcher-bearers worked heroically, but they couldn't do impossibilities. Stretcher-bearers are not a little looked down upon by a certain type of loose thinker and ready talker; I have heard and seen them sniffed at rather disdainfully. But not by soldiers; ye gods, no! We know them. We have seen them at work. But some shallow-pated civilians are apt to class them as an inferior sort of soldier. Well, for my part, I think infinitely more highly of the non-combatant who takes his life in his hand and goes to risk it at the edge of the cauldron than I do of the non-combatant who stays at home snug, and talks much. It is easier to talk in Pall Mall than it is to carry wounded men through fire, under a hot sun, or, in the dark, across dangerous, unknown hostile territory. 'They also serve who only stand and wait' is eloquently true of life at the front, and the service of the stretcher-bearer is as fine and as brave as anything men ever do. It requires a great amount of coolness and bravery to be a useful stretcher-bearer. And I never saw one funk or fail. In the attack there is always a tense excitement that stimulates and carries you. Even the feeling of 'For Heaven's sake, let's keep moving!' which most soldiers know and many voice, though in itself a form of nervousness, is a spur and a help, and because of it you grip your rifle or revolver tight and look for your foe. The stretcher-bearers, on the other hand, have to go about prosaically looking for the wounded, rendering first aid, and paying no attention to the shells screaming and the bullets whizzing all about them. That takes some doing. Try it and see. It takes twice as much pluck to be shot at and keep your nerve when you can't shoot back. And in the confounded peninsula the shot and the shell never seemed to cease whizzing and spitting and pounding. When the bearers got hold of a wounded man, taking him down to the advanced dressing-station was an intolerably difficult job. The constant, haphazard, crisscross gun-fire made it dangerous; the extraordinary formation of the surface of the blessed place made it almost impossible. It is preposterous to say that the stretcher-bearers had it any easier than we had at the Dardanelles.

I was much concerned over a subaltern who had been shot through the head. If, by a miracle, anything could be done for him, he must be got away at once. Captain Wilson, though wounded, managed to get hold of two waterproof sheets. We tied them together, and he started off with two men carrying the wounded subaltern. At the front it is not an extraordinary sight to see wounded carrying wounded; and as for wounded leaning on wounded, wounded leading wounded, you see them all the time.

The party got to an Australian dressing-station, but it was full up there twice over, and no attention could be gained for the boy. The bearers took him up and went on with him. Luckily they found our regimental M.O., who fixed him up temporarily. Eventually he was got to the beach, and from there to Alexandria. His star was in the ascendant now, wound or no wound, for the bugler-boy mentioned before was in the same ship. Wounded and suffering though he was, for three days and nights that bugler nursed the lieutenant as only a rough, untrained soldier can nurse the officer he loves.

The subaltern lived. I saw him a month later in hospital. He looked very ill still, and chalky; but he was as cheerful as a schoolboy on a holiday. He is in Scotland now, able to go about and use his limbs and his life normally. It was, I think, an absolute triumph of mind over body. He was terribly wounded. He suffered frightfully. But not for one instant did he lose even a shade of his natural cheerfulness. To be shot through the brain is fatal on the spot almost always – certainly in ninety-nine cases out of a hundred, I suppose. I have heard of several very wonderful recoveries, but of no other quite so extraordinary.

The doctors, the surgeons, the nurses (I hold my bonnet in my hand as I write of the army nurse), and the hospitals have done a great deal for our forces in this supreme war, and it would be impossible to exaggerate, or even to hint, what they have done. I believe that the war has done even more for medical science and for that drastic mercy which we call 'surgery.' Indeed, under this war's tutelage medicine, nursing, and surgery have become no longer only science – they have become miracle. If some great physician with the graphic pen that often twins the skilful scalpel would write the story of the recoveries of this war's wounded, 'shocked', and invalided, it would be the greatest war-book ever written, and the most marvellous.

The battle was still raging, but I had an hour's rest in the afternoon, and then we had unexpected orders to advance again.

I believe that I am as devoid of superstition as any self-respecting Scotsman can be without feeling a wee bit naked. But more than once at the front I have run up against queer things, uncanny facts that I could not understand, and cannot. And the more, and the more coolly, I think of them, the more impossible of common-sense explanation they seem. Here is an instance – call it premonition, call it what you like; explain it, if you can. About half-an-hour before the orders came one of our few remaining subalterns, who happened to be sitting beside me, said, 'I feel that I am going to be hit to-night.'

'Nonsense, Paterson!' I retorted; 'we are not going to move to-night.'

'Yes,' he persisted, 'I am sure we are. And I'm booked for a bullet. I know it – I sort of see it. The funny thing is, I don't seem particularly to mind. And I think it isn't much.'

Well, the orders came, and at half-past six Paterson went over with the first wave.

The second wave had gone on, and I was watching a ridge, about five hundred yards in front, which I didn't like the look of, when I saw the first wave reach it. And then – they simply melted away. They went down like ninepins, to a man. It was my turn now to go on; so I had a spurt for a trench two hundred yards ahead. I gained it, and in it I found the C.O.

The second wave had just got to the ridge now. Most of it melted away as the first had; and the C.O. determined to send the remnant a message to dig in where they were, and be ready to retire at night to our position, which was much better and more easily consolidated.

I turned to find a messenger, and I met Paterson coming over the top of the trench with a bullet through his shoulder. I think he was grateful to that bullet, pleased to get out of it for a bit, and I don't blame him. 'I told you so!' he said as he passed on. A commonplace story. You've heard some hundreds like it since August 1914? Precisely! And that is what makes it so significant.

I began to wonder when my turn was coming. But I was too busy to think much about it and too tired and hungry to care particularly. It was eight now, and another day had gone by with precious little to eat. I was just starting off to have a forage round, when a brigade major of the Australians, who were on our left, arrived to say that they would have to retire. That was a trifle upsetting, for it meant that our left flank would be in the air, and it was ten to one that Mr Abdul Turk would come prowling round that way. He prowls a great deal, especially after dusk.

We hadn't telephone communication with headquarters at the beginning, and for the present we had really lost touch with it; our orderlies were getting so knocked about that we had no one to send back and forward. There is a great deal of running back and forth m active service, and especially in actual battle. Science and invention have regulated and minimised this, as they have regulated and simplified everything else, and it makes my legs ache to think what the to and fro of it must have been in pre-'phone campaigns. But those wars were so much less intricate in most ways, and their stages so much smaller, that perhaps it all balanced.

It seemed to me that, since this was my job, I'd better get to headquarters (if I could) and give them the message, as it appeared important that something should be done, and done soon. The C.O. agreed with me, and off I went. It was dark now. I took a rifle, and hopped off to the nullah, which was, I thought, about a hundred and fifty yards to our right rear. With my usual luck (did I tell you I was born on a Friday?), the nightly fusillade and I started together. So I had to sprint lustily for about fifty yards, and then recline as flat as I could on the cold, cold ground and get my breath. Hopping is not a soldierly gait, but it was the only possible sprinting-gait in that nutmeg-grater of a place, all holes and spikes. If, in the days of drill at home, we could have seen the configuration of this theatre of our future military achievements, we should not have grumbled at P.T. exercise. The hopping exercises came in with peculiar usefulness at Gallipoli.

This was my first essay at running about in the dark. I had almost hopped my feet off, hop-hopping about the blessed peninsula, and I had grown a callus on my back (it's there yet – permanently, I think) by lying down suddenly and long on the flinty ridges of the sun-cracked earth when the bullets began to pelt; but I had done it by daylight, when I could see where I was hopping or flopping.

I did not enjoy myself a bit. The bullets were bouncing in and out of the ground all about me. Twice they scratched my boot, and I couldn't find the nullah. I was just about fed-up with myself, the war, and every one, when things took a poignant turn. A voice just in front of me shouted, 'Halt! Hands up!' I halted very slick. You usually do. But I didn't put up my hands. I wasn't long in doing so, though, when I discovered a well-pointed revolver about six inches from my stomach. My challenger proved to be an officer with whom I had come out. I had run in a semicircle, and had arrived back at the firing-line, but away on our right, and at another regiment's sector.

I asked him if he could direct me to headquarters. He pointed to three lights out at sea, and told me to march on the centre one; so off I hopped once more, munching some biscuits I had commandeered, for I was infernally hungry by now. Hopping in the dark, and munching biscuits as I hopped! Not a very soldierly picture? I beg your pardon, that is just what it is. War is not all purple and plumes and stately, burnished dignity. Oh no!

I hadn't gone very far when I thought I heard footsteps. I wasn't taking any needless chances – foolhardiness was bad taste in Gallipoli – so down I flopped behind a whin-bush, and clicked a cartridge into my breech. A figure sauntered into view. So I had a go at, 'Halt! Hands up!'

'All right, guv'nor,' came the friendly reply. The Anzacs take to 'sir' about as naturally as they do to saluting. This one was a stretcher-bearer, no tunic on, his shirt-sleeves rolled up to his armpits, his trousers rolled up above his knees, 'just having a look round' for wounded. All the time we were at the Dardanelles I seemed never to see an Australian stretcher-bearer that was not working. Well, there was always work for them to find and to do.

I asked this chap if he knew where the 88th Brigade Headquarters were. He did not; but he said that there was a dressing-station close by on my right, and that I should see its light a little farther on. I found the station, a sort of farmhouse; but every one was too busy to pay the slightest attention to me, so off I went again on my lonesome own. I soon came to a trench, but there was no one at home. I helped myself to a bit of bully-beef, a biscuit, and a drink of Adam's ale, and pounded on. My next small adventure was an encounter with two Pathans. The moon had come out just then, and I saw clearly that they were Indians, and so didn't bother with any more 'Hands up!' but got at once to my eternal question, 'Can you tell me where the headquarters of' —

'No talk Englishe. Talk Hindustani,' one of the tall fellows interrupted me.

I have my accomplishments, but the 'talking' of Hindustani is not among them. I resumed my weary walk, mentally anathematising everybody in general, and not a little worried about the regiment, for the Very lights were going strong, and so was the rifle-fire.

A few more wrong turns, a few more small adventures, and suddenly, just as I was getting downright heartsick, I walked 'slap-bang' into the very man I was looking for – our brigade major. And I was within eighty yards of headquarters. I pitched him my anxious tale, and he rushed me in to the general, who got on to the 'phone to the division, and things were fixed up.

The general asked me whether I could take the brigade major back with me. I said that I thought I could, so – right-about turn and off we went, in single file, the brigade major leading with revolver cocked, I close at his heels, his orderly close at mine.

The major turned his head to speak to me, and caught sight of my wrist-watch, which had a luminous face. 'Take that damned thing off!'

he ordered sharply. I meekly did, and shoved it into my pocket. I had been hopping all over the end of the peninsula with it dancing like a fire-fly on my wrist, the more shame to me. He had spotted it on the instant. His ultra-precaution was in no way misplaced. The older and abler the soldier, the greater his caution. That is one of the few rules that have no exception.

We could see dimly various figures moving about in the dusk. Most of them were the Colonial stretcher-bearers, pushing about here, there, and everywhere at their never-ending toil. They were the ferrets of our army, after-the-battle ferrets of mercy – though Heaven knows they worked in the battle also. Its scorch never stayed them a moment, and Heaven, I make no doubt, records it.

After sundry small episodes, we contrived to get back to my friend who had greeted me with his pistol. He directed us to push on to our left until we came to a small gap not yet filled up, and there, he said, we should find my own trench.

I started to be guide now, and we went merrily on. We found the gap, but no trench. I found instead (and almost walked the three of us into it) a small lagoon I had never seen before in my life. I called a halt and confessed we were lost. At that moment the machine-guns shifted their fire into our quarter. We lay flat on our stomachs for one horrid hour, and then we grew desperate and very full of stomach-ache, and began to crawl back to the wood. We reached it – and my friend – still in single file, wriggling ignominiously on our bellies, just as the old, old serpent was condemned to wriggle out of Eden.

I was past worrying now, and just wriggled on mechanically, doing my crawling utmost, my lowly duty, but not caring much how it ended. I was half-dead for sleep. Suddenly I remembered at last where the small donga was that I usually used as my landmark when returning 'home' from one of my constant wanderings. So the major and I started off to find it. And we did find it. I got the place without much difficulty. I knew that one of our dumps was there, and located it, and knocked up a quartermaster-sergeant, who led us to the fire-trench. It was just 3 a.m. I think the C.O. was glad to see us. I know I was glad to see 'home'. We three discussed the position for an hour or more, and then the brigade major left. He made his return journey safely, and at its end, as he jumped into his dug-out, he was shot. He was badly wounded, but I believe he recovered finally.

I discovered the next day that we had been gaily crawling into the Turkish lines, and but for the lucky accident of finding the lagoon, we should probably soon have been sojourning as prisoners on an island in the Sea of Marmora.

I took an hour's rest. I should have lain down longer, if fewer people had walked over me. But fewer people did not, so up I got and began my day's work. It started with burying our dead. I was anxious to get it done, out of decent respect to them, and for our own sake too. But it was dangerous work today, and I had to postpone it. The snipers were far too busy. I was standing close to three men who were digging a grave for two poor fellows, brothers, when the digger nearest me sank down at my feet, saying, 'Oh sir, I'm shot!' And shot he was through his shoulder. I stopped the burying-party, and we dragged him into the trench.

The sentry on duty where we dropped into the trench looked over the parapet and exclaimed, 'I think he's in that bush, sir.' Like a fool, I looked over too, and instantly up spurted the earth, and a stone none so small struck me on the cheek. I turned round with my hand to my face, and I saw that the poor sentry was gasping his last. You can't be too careful when snipers are about. They are the very devil to deal with.

They are difficult to spot, and you can't organise parties to hunt them in daylight within five hundred yards of the enemy's trenches.

Having had quite enough tragedy for one day, I went off to see where and what my breakfast was. I don't think I'd had a decent meal for three days. In fact, I couldn't remember when I had eaten anything more exciting or savoury than biscuits munched here and there as I went. It is wonderful what you can exist on when you are tuned up to concert-pitch. Warfare makes you very hungry – ravenous – when you have time to realise it, but you have time only now and then; and far more than it makes you hungry, war makes you oddly independent of food. Excitement is food in itself – I suppose that is the explanation of the long fasts of zealots, mystics, and adepts – but nature gets her own back later.

I made a huge breakfast, and then I snuggled down on a nice bed of dirt, and fell asleep to the terrible lullaby of the guns. I do not mention the guns constantly, but constantly the guns were belching and thundering. The noise in Gallipoli rose and fell, but it never died. It rarely slept. We grew used to it, and when silence came it startled and hurt. It was only silence that made our ears ache.

Good news was coming. It reached us at six that afternoon. We were to be relieved. Then the order was cancelled. That was too much. The men were just about played out. Every human creature has a breaking-point. Even the steel nerve of a Titan can wear thin. They were still as game as could be, as game as they'd been from the first. But they had done enough – for a spell. Half of them, of those left to us, had had eighteen days and nights of fighting, and the other half for the first seven days had been running ammunition and stores to the beach, to the big-bellied beast of Gallipoli that gulped down hecatombs of men, stores, munitions, guns, and then hiccoughed for more! The stores and ammunition running was dangerous and exciting enough, Heaven knows, but you had always a ship to go to, and no chance of a counter-attack.

I had not had my boots off for twelve days, or my clothes. I thought that my shirt had grown into my flesh in more than one place, and I knew that every inch of my skin was riddled with bites. In the twelve days I had shaved twice, and had washed, in a quart or less of water, just three times. For the rest – I had merely shaken myself like a dog, and had longed for a dog's other methods of cleanliness, and had regretted itchingly that the peninsula of Gallipoli was not, like Korea, provided every few rods with a scratching-post.

'I shall never make a good soldier,' one of our subalterns said to me bitterly one day, a boy who had already done two of the bravest things that were done at the Dardanelles.

'If you're fishing for compliments, fish elsewhere,' I retorted.

'Compliments be blowed! I mean it. There are details of active service I never could assimilate, and can scarcely endure. To die for one's country is all very well, and simple enough if it comes along in your day's work. But to itch for your country, day in and night out, for three weeks on end – that takes the patriotism of a super-saint, and demands the hide of a rhinoceros.'

And I think he was right.

About eight o'clock glorious news came. A pink paper was delivered to the C.O. 'The 5th Royal Scots will be relieved tomorrow morning by orders of the G.O.C. Hooray! hooray! *That* can't be cancelled, can it?'

'I hope not, sir,' I said fervently. And I meant it.

Further orders came saying where we were to rest, or, rather, be supposed to rest. Rest! It wasn't done in Gallipoli.

The cooks were sent off with a fatigue-party that night, in order that breakfast might be ready on the battalion's arrival the next morning.

It was my job to leave before the relieving, so at half-past three in the morning I stepped off with an orderly. The dawn was just breaking.

After the first half-mile, as it was fairly safe, I eased up and lit my pipe. I felt at peace with *all* the world, though all the world was at war; all the world was at war, and I had cause to know that it was.

It was a lovely dawn. Everything felt inexpressibly fresh. The new day was a bath. The birds were peeping and chirping. The frogs were croaking companionably. My orderly began to whistle 'Roy's Wife of Aldi-valloch'. And between the puffings of my pipe I began to hum. Out at sea the island of Imbros blinked and glistened, and it might have been the Arran hills, and we, my orderly and I, going a-maying on the west coast, so like was this to that.

I have rarely been happier. I can recall no other hour so perfectly peaceful. There can be, I think, no other relief so complete, so satisfying to soul and to body, no other relief comparable to the reliefs from battle. We had come out of hell. But this was peace, perfect peace. We were famished, and we were going to eat abundant food in cleanliness and at leisure. We had been in deadly peril. We were safe. I was vermin-ridden and sweat-stenched. As I walked I could feel the unclean moisture caked between my toes. My feet felt like morasses of mud. But I was going to rest and be clean. Best of all, I was going to have my fill of sleep – sleep secure, uncurtailed, uninterrupted:

The innocent sleep;
Sleep, that knits up the ravell'd sleeve of care,
The death of each day's life, sore labour's bath,
Balm of hurt minds, great nature's second course,
Chief nourisher in life's feast.

I once heard a very learned scholar 'prove' that Shakespeare was at one time a soldier, claiming it not so much because the acceptance of that theory would fill up a blank in what we know of the poet's years, as because of the master's descriptions of soldiering; and in the British Museum there is a little book to the same effect, 'caviare to the general', but treasured of the adepts.

I am convinced that Shakespeare never was a soldier. Had he been, he must have written more adequately of war. I do not say that he would have written adequately of battle. That is not to be done. Twenty Shakespeares could not do it. But he has described war and warfare most inadequately; and if to say so is sacrilege, that sacrilege is mine.

For instance, Macbeth was a soldier – would he have left out from his great apostrophe all mention of the soldier's sleep? It is unthinkable. But all that Macbeth said of sleep, I felt in blissful anticipation as I smoked and hummed my happy way to the rest-camp. 'Sore labour's bath.' By Heaven! it's that, is sleep. Probably no other two torments, no other two strains, are so strangely and strongly alike as are the tumult and the strain of childbirth and of battle; the torment and the strain that bring man into life, to cuddle and smile and drink on a mother's warm white breast, and the torment and the strain that hack men to death wholesale, and leave them to rot untended on an alien field, or unshrouded in unknown graves. And to the young mother who gives life for love's sake, and the soldier who takes life for hatred's or for duty's sake, sleep must come sweetest, most blessed of all, I think.

We were going to food, rest, and sleep, and our souls purred like contented cats as we went our way in the flower-scented sunrise. Even the guns in the distance whispered drowsily, and had a soothing, friendly sound.

Chapter 14

The Rest Camp

It is not inappropriate, I think, to quote here General Sir Ian Hamilton's Order of the Day. Naturally we were very proud of it, and it gives an authoritative idea of what we had passed through.

'Special Order of the Day.
'General Headquarters, 9th May 1915.

'Sir Ian Hamilton wishes the troops of the Mediterranean Expeditionary Force to be informed that in all his past experiences, which include the hard struggles of the Russo-Japanese campaign, he has never seen more devoted gallantry displayed than this which has characterised their efforts during the past three days. He has informed Lord Kitchener by cable of the bravery and endurance displayed by all ranks here, and has asked that the necessary reinforcements be forthwith despatched. Meanwhile the remainder of the East Lancashire Division is disembarking, and will henceforth be available to help us to make good and improve upon the positions we have so hardly won.

'E. M. Woodward,

Brigadier-General,
Deputy Adjutant-General, M.E.F.'

It was still very early when we arrived at the rest-camp, but already the cooks were plying industriously their savoury art, and even before I bathed, I breakfasted. Oh! it was good to sit alone and eat clean food, smoking hot, well cooked, and to eat it at leisure. To crown all, they found me a tin of 'Aberdeen haddies'. It was such a change getting a peaceful meal that I could scarcely believe it was I.

When I had eaten, I washed. When I had washed, I slept.

It was nine that same morning when they woke me, saying that the battalion was in sight. I went to watch it coming, and the men as they came in. I was very much struck with their faces. Those who had been boys when we sailed into the Aegean were men now, adolescence scorched and destroyed in the heat of war, their young mouths set and stern from the strain of having gone through hell. Some of them I hardly recognised – and I had known them well, seen them daily. Their very being seemed changed utterly, their souls new forged, their faces for ever seared.

On the whole, these – ours – were physically smaller men than the magnificent men of the Regular battalions of the division; but they were stout of heart – for ever hurt by what they had seen, by what they had borne, but game to the backbone. I could not tell a hundredth part of what those Gallipoli days had already been. I would not if I could. Oh! the British race is not decadent yet. The 'flannelled fool's' a hero. And the men more immediately of the people are whelped of lions, and should beget lion whelps. Britain has no need to be ashamed of her sons yet. There'll be no repetition of history by the falling of our Empire as the Empire of the Romans fell. That stood proved to the blood-drenched hilt when a raw little army of contemptible amateurs did what that army did, when a regiment of amateur soldiers (with perhaps a dozen exceptions, certainly not more) – mainly youngsters

– students, clerks, tradesmen – after six months' training fought as they fought, died as they died, went down into the inferno at Gallipoli, faced death with a smile, and accepted it too, not for themselves, not for gain as gain is counted, but to uphold British freedom.

We may often muddle things a bit. But isn't it better to 'muddle through' than to make a big white-and-gold dash, boast of God Himself as our ally, ride over Europe roughshod, and fall at the last ditch?

Our Tommies nicknamed that rest-camp 'The Baths'. And certainly we all bathed. We could not have needed to do so worse than we did. There was a small stream near by. The men made a dam in it. And soon a regiment could be seen naked and unashamed. We officers had few luxuries at the Dardanelles. Valises we had not yet seen, and goodness knows where they were now. However, you soon get used to having only a pack. Some of us had not even that. I had a change of underclothing in mine, so I soon felt like a new being. The clothes I took off I handled gingerly, and laid them carefully, well spread out, in the sunshine – which was supposed to drive away vermin. I took off my boots with trepidation, vastly exercised lest I should never get them on again, but have to finish the campaign in my bare feet.

It was rather funny passing up the line, seeing men, in every conceivable sort of get-up or in none, having a good old 'hunt'. Monkeys weren't in it!

Barring those who attended to the few duties that had to be done, I think that every one slept the clock round. And some slept before they ate and washed. When the regiment was marched in and dismissed, many a man fell on his face as he stood, and slept as he fell; worn out quite, and soothed, by the relaxation of torturing strain, to instant slumber, as peaceful as a baby's. So far as we possibly could, we let such sleepers lie undisturbed. We were 'kind to ane anither' in

Gallipoli rest-camp. Unfortunately my duties permitted me no such luxury, at least at the moment; for the usual confounded returns had to be sent to headquarters with peace-time promptness. Red tape is never needlessly loosened on active service. And I am convinced that this is as it should be. Red tape is a much-misabused article. It binds. It supports. Any number of important things would slip and slide about, get misplaced and lost, if the discipline of red tape were loosened. All praise to red tape, say I for one. But while I must praise and revere it, still I hate it. Like Mr Kipling's Atkins, I am no plaster saint, and after this war is over, I hope, if I am still here, never to see or hear the words 'For information and necessary action'; and if I chance to go over the Big Top, my last prayer on earth and my first petition beyond the Styx'll be: 'Don't make me an adjutant in heaven, or – somewhere else.'

Our C.O. was no disbeliever in red tape and such any more than I am, and he decided the next day that discipline would have to be re-maintained rigorously. There is nothing else that so tunes and tones the men. It may not be his favourite tipple, but it's Tommy's tonic, every time.

The following day the C.O., Captain M'Lagan, ordered church services. There had been none since we landed, and this seemed a fitting time for those of us left – not quite half of us now – to return thanks.

Our padre, who had joined us in Egypt, came from Dunedin, New Zealand. It was a pleasant coincidence that that far-off town, named after Scotland's capital, should have sent an Edinburgh regiment its padre. He was a topping chap. I suspect he'd rather have been a combatant. He was always strolling up to the firing-line and lounging about there as if he liked the smoky smell and the warm breeze of the place. And wandering in the open in Gallipoli was no sanatorium stunt. We didn't run to communication trenches in those days. But he was every inch a priest, and many anguished wounded, many a passing soul, must have hailed him, 'Oh, comfortable Friar!' He was a 'brick' and a man.

Where to have the services was a question. Not even here (or in any place in Gallipoli that I know) could you gather a body of men together without their being *almost instantly* shelled. At last we selected a spot, neither too far nor too near, under the frail shelter of a few trees, and there we held two services, sending half the battalion at a time. Most of the men were Presbyterians, and these two principal services were theirs. The Roman Catholics went a little later to Mass in the French lines. The Church of England members joined an English regiment's service the next Sunday, but I think most of them had already gone to the alfresco 'kirk'. Men rarely shun church or chapel at the front.

We never held another service in the daylight. It was too risky. The few others that we held were at night.

It was very impressive, listening to the old hymns sung at dark, in the Turkish open, stars for far-off candles just pricking the black of night with their promise of light to come, and their twinkled reminder that 'over the stars there is rest'. It was heart-felt singing that we throated to the Aegean night, prayers sung to Heaven, soldiers' thoughts of home, with whiffs of a neighbouring field of scent-heavy, Eastern night-flowers for incense. It was a grave and a tender service. It made one quiet, and it made one thoughtful.

In the morning I decided to manoeuvre myself a day off, and to meander down to dear old Beach W to see how things had progressed there. Some excuse had to be made. I foraged about in the store cupboard of my head, and found two quite creditable excuses. I had thirty-four golden sovereigns tied up in a dirty handkerchief. It seemed to be getting near my turn to get knocked out, and if I were, my bits of gold might fall into the coffers of the Turk. Clearly it seemed my duty to get that soiled handkerchief into the keeping of our field cashier, and he was somewhere on the beach. Evidently several men of our unit were wandering about the beach, through no fault of their own, not engaged in prescribed activities, and I had just had a peculiarly nasty chit about it from headquarters. It seemed imperative that I should investigate personally and promptly.

I got permission, and trotted down to the beach. I hardly recognised the place. It was incredibly changed. It looked as if we had been there for years. If Jack's a handy man, Tommy's a wonderful housemaid. And, by Jove! we British may be muddlers, but we're great organisers. Everthing was going like clockwork now on Beach W; and when I had seen it last, not quite ten days before, it was a quagmire of tangle, an inferno of disorder, that would have overtaxed the pen of Dante.

I found the field cashier dug into a hole in the cliff – the rummiest bank you ever saw. He was delighted to get the sovereigns. The financial greed of your working patriot is almost indecent; there is no selfish personal greed that compares with it. He gave me a receipt, which I sent to Alexandria the next day. So one small hoard was safe from the foe.

I took a look round for any of my men, and I found several. They all seemed to be working, and each said he was doing what he had been ordered to do. So off I went to see the camp commandant who had recently come to boss the beach. I found his 'quarters', and in them I unearthed another of my men, working away on a typewriter and looking confoundedly pleased with himself. In the midst of war he and his spick-and-span instrument made a charming picture of peace.

I said nothing, but kept him and his alphabet-organ for use as a *quid pro quo*. The commandant arrived on the scene, and I told him that I was getting strafed for some of my men being on the beach when they should be in the firing-line. I had discovered a number of them, I told him, sunning themselves in cushy jobs, for which they apparently had been commandeered by various 'brass hats'. He was mildly and discreetly sympathetic, and promised to go into the matter. But the tone in which he promised lacked the sterling ring of enthusiasm. So I played my *quid pro quo*, and remarked incidentally that he had one of my most useful men working as his clerk. That did it. I got my men, and left him the typing expert, who, after all, was pretty seedy. He was a nice chap, and he was perfectly brave, but I guess he was quite comfy where he was.

It is wonderful how a man falls into his niche if he strongly wishes to, even in the peremptory stress and the curtailed fields of active service. I had an orderly in Scotland who always turned up to do orderly duty notwithstanding that the orderlies were frequently changed, so that none of them should be skimped of his due of training and drill. I got tired of this chap's persistent and unquenchable orderlyhood, and sent him back to his company. Two days later I ran across him – he was assisting with the musketry stores. I had him pushed out of that. Four days later I was inspecting the cookhouses, and I discovered that my friend was now a cook. That conquered me. Any man that would rather wear a bib and apron and flourish a long-handled spoon than work a gun or wield a sword ought, in my disgusted opinion, to be allowed to do so. And his company commander said that he was no use at drill, 'So I made him a cook.'

'Can he cook?' I asked.

'He can cook better than he can drill,' was the C.O.'s acidulated reply. So as a cook he went to the front (no, not the company commander).

In the afternoon the guns on the Asiatic side played a brisk tattoo on Beach W, as they always did at short intervals. It was annoying, but this time their slaughter was scarcely worth the cost of their shells. They killed just one mule.

Towards evening the cooks' wagons started off with rations, and I got a lift back to the rest-camp. My day on W Beach had been a pleasant break.

W Beach a pleasant break! That is eloquent! If any one had told me! Well, well! 'We know what we are,' some of us, 'but we know not what we may be,' any of us.

Our rest-camp wasn't the picnic we had anticipated. It was more camp than rest. We had several casualties there. Think of being shot at all the time and hit occasionally while doing a rest-cure in a nursing-home! It was the long-range bullets of the Turk that made our camp restless and a poor place of repose. And they are nasty things, long-range bullets. They get into all sorts of odd places in a man. And once inside human flesh, they turn the veriest nomads, and journey about mysteriously in your odd corners all on their own. They won't come out, if they can help it. They are the devil and all to find, and the wounded man gets terribly knocked about before they are located. There were no easy-chairs in that rest-camp, and no eider-downs, and it lacked elegance. But it was sweeter than the firing-line.

You were never free from something while you were in the peninsula, no matter where you were – on the earth or in it, on the sea or in it, or in the air. If it wasn't bullets, it was shells. If it wasn't shells, it was colic. If it wasn't fever, it was chill; and often it was both. And the fleas we had always with us.

But it is wonderful what you can put up with, when you have to.

A pink paper fluttered in at about eight o'clock that evening, saying that we were to be inspected the next morning by Major-General Sir Hunter Weston, the G.O.C. the 29th Division. We hurried to bed, to get as much sleep as we could that we might seem fresh and brisk when our general came. Rough men, some rough from birth, all roughened and shabby from war, stained and tattered from battle, we were as elated and as anxious as a bevy of girls going to their first dance, because our general was coming. Pathetic? Yes, I think it was pathetic, and I likewise think it was fine.

At dawn the next day the first rain I had seen since I left England came down. It was no 'gentle rain from heaven'. It pelted us as the Turks never had. It was so vicious, so relentless, that it might have been every drop German and we helpless women and children. It bombarded and soaked us. It spoilt the whole show. But the general said a lot of nice things, as the water dripped off his hat on to his nose.

The rain went as suddenly as it came. A scorching sun came out and cooked the ground dry in a few hours. And that very afternoon we started sending working-parties off to make roads. We needed the roads, but that was only our minor reason for attempting to make them. It was vitally important to keep the men occupied, and they could do no drill without being potted at – and hit.

The Church of England padre came to us the next day. He held a Communion Service. I shall never forget it. For I am an Episcopalian, and was there. The scene was passing strange. In a small field under the half-shelter of a little copse, a hundred khaki figures were silently kneeling. The priest, wearing his surplice, stood at an altar made of two boxes – one had held cheese, the other had held soap. They were covered with our flag. There was a cross on the altar – a cross of wild flowers. And in the grassy nave poppies and nodding plumy grasses grew. The Aegean Sea smiled and watched us. It was scarcely a mile away, and as blue as the Virgin's own robes. And near by, on that old sea, the Greek islands, many of which are mentioned in the Bible, looked like jewelled caskets of green.

The general commanding the brigade was there with his staff. Almost it might have been an open-air service at home during one of our trainings in peace-time. But the faces of the men belied that. They were wonderful faces, with the indescribable look of those who have journeyed far and seen much, and in their eyes was that grave, far-away look that tells both of mental strain and of vision, both of pain and of endurance.

After the short service the priest passed to each of the silent figures, giving us the bread and the wine. We ate and we drank; then we covered our faces in prayer.

Chapter 15

Back to the Fir-Tree Wood

After one more day came orders for us to go back to the firing-line, and so, for the time being, our so-called rest was over.

It had not been a halcyon time, but it had had its points, and to us one of the pleasantest of them was the issuing of another order of the day which ran:

'Special Order.

'General Headquarters,
18th May 1916.

'For the first time for eighteen days and nights it has been found possible to withdraw the 29th Division from the fire fight. During the whole of that long period of unprecedented strain the division had held ground or gained it against the bullets and bayonets of the constantly renewed forces of the foe. During the whole of that long period they have been illuminating the pages of military history with their blood. The losses have been terrible, but mingling with the deep sorrow for fallen comrades arises a feeling of pride in the invincible spirit which has enabled the survivors to triumph where ordinary troops must inevitably have failed. I tender to Major-General Hunter Weston and to his division at the same time my profoundest sympathy with their losses and my warmest congratulations on their achievement.

'Ian Hamilton,
General.'

We had come into rest-camp jubilantly, all of us, though some had had to crawl, and some had dropped and slept as they came. We went back very gravely. I believe the second going into battle is much harder than the first. The man who has lived through even one action knows; the man who has as yet been in none cannot even imagine. War beggars all imagination, as it beggars all description. We went back gravely.

We left the camp about dusk, that we might arrive at the firing-line when it was dark. It was my first experience of relieving trenches. Now much practice has made me a little more facile in this, which at best is difficult and anxious work. But then a few hours of it tired me more than a day's fighting did. In those first Gallipoli days we had no communication-trenches, and it took very little to upset the best-made plans, and to deadlock in a nasty tangle the men that were coming out and the men that were going in. And it was important that the relief should be done with the utmost noiselessness.

On arriving near the firing-line I discovered, to my disgust, that we were going back to that pernicious Fir-Tree Wood. The trenches had not been much improved since I was there before. In one of them I found two regiments packed like herrings in a barrel, so tight that the only way to budge them threatened to be to prise the men out one by one with a knife. I made them lie down flat and crawl along the top of the rear, protected only by the parapet. (The dignity of warfare is often more honoured in the breach than in the observance. Many a detachment has crawled on its belly, worm-like, to victory.) The enemy, thank goodness, happened to be quiet for once, and after a strenuous struggle we managed the relief, but it was mighty near the dawn before we did!

However, we had only two casualties going up, and not one when actually relieving; otherwise I don't believe that Odysseus in his shining armour and with his singing bow could have saved the situation.

I will not describe our first night in our trench. I wish I might forget it!

After breakfast we addressed ourselves to improving the trenches, for there seemed no prospect of an imminent advance. So far it had never been possible to have an officers' mess. It was getting rather tiresome having people endeavouring to walk over your head just as you were guiding a cup of tea to your lips – and heavily shod people at that. We decided unanimously that we'd have an officers' mess of some sort. And we had it.

There was a sort of bank at about the centre of our position. We dug into this bank, and made an earthen table. An officers' mess might have been more private. But this was the Dardanelles campaign. Our alcove was open on its longest side to all who went along the trench. We sat on three sides only of our unfestal board – at each end, and on the long side nearest the outer wall. There were only six effective officers of us now, but we often had a guest. (We had some whisky.) The men, of course, passed up and down the trench freely, at our meal-hours as at all other hours. They had to; it was their only thoroughfare.

Our first afternoon here a box arrived from home. We gathered about it like boys about a box of 'tuck'. In many ways we were rather like boys, and well for us and for our cause that we were; we could not else have endured to the end. By this time our mess had been landed. It had been well and generously packed before leaving England. Between it and the tuck-box a man's wife had sent, we were able to show quite a spread, and a fine glitter and litter of tins piled on the floor of our ungilded recess, for that mud-carpeted floor was the only larder we had. We used to have dinner about half-past six. A long communication-trench had been cut now on the left of our mess, and several regiments often passed our table on their way to relieve other regiments on our right. It was amusing to hear the remarks of the men. A slight curve in the trench hid us from their view longer than it hid our stores. 'Blimey, Bill, who owns the picnic? Our orficers does their bloomin' sel's bloomin' well! Co-ome on; I've picked a damned fine tin o' something up, lad. Help yersel' to a square one o' Johnny Walker. – Good old Johnny! Glad to see yer, proud to know yer, John, me boy. I say, Johnny, me boy, does yer mother know ye're out? Ye're a damned long way from her. Come right along with me, dear.' But our mess corporal being a dour Scotsman, Johnny Walker was not allowed to walk out with Mr Thomas Atkins. Suddenly the men, a few steps nearer now, would see that there were officers there, and an avalanche of stone-dead silence would fall, to be broken by gleeful titters that were sternly checked by the non-coms.

It had now been decided by the Higher Command that open warfare was to cease, temporarily at least, and that trench warfare should begin in deadliest earnest. This meant driving out saps and connecting them. The men did not relish this mode of fighting. They loathed it – and, for the matter of that, so did we. But it was safer, though infinitely harder work physically, than battling in the open, desperately hard as we had found that. And now we had the telephone through to headquarters. That saved a lot of trouble, especially for me, for I still had the charming job of returns.

Near at hand a few Turks that would never fight again were lying about, strangely peaceable, but decidedly odoriferous. And just behind them was a dead mule. It became absolutely necessary to get it buried. So a party was detailed to remove it and inter it somehow. There were no volunteers – not one. Men whom I had seen dash over the top cheerfully, almost gaily, funked this. But they obeyed the definite order when I gave it, obeyed it wryly, and their awful job was accomplished somehow. I forbore to ask how or where. The mule was bad, but a Turk is really smelly, and the hot sun does not improve such situations. One gets used to anything in war, but I think that the acrid, pungent odour of the unburied dead, which gets into your very mouth, down your tortured throat, and seems even to taint and taste your food, is really the worst thing you have to face on active service. And you have to face several things at which heroism itself must wince, and may wince without shame. Before long you grow quite inured, if not indifferent even, to the sight of the unburied dead. But to the death smell no one can grow used or callous. Rot and decay and the stench of putrefaction are the supreme and the final degradation of our flesh. And the uncontrollable nausea that the smell of the dead too long unburied must cause the living is not, I believe, solely a physical nausea. But, except through one's nostrils, one grows steeled, if not dense and heartless. You see horrible sights which in peace-time would make your gorge rise uncontainably, and you take them, in the swelter of war, as a matter of course. I have seen men in the trenches making a fire and cooking their bacon close to the corpse of a comrade who had 'gone West' not a yard away, not an hour before, and who had shared their last meal with them.

Death is our commonplace on active service, and Tommy accepts and regards it as casually as the grocer deals with his soap, the gardener with his guano. One might think that men become brutes, their finer instincts blunted and rasped quite away, in the lust of killing. But that is not so. For nowhere will you find a more sympathetic creature than our private soldier is to his wounded pal – and they are all pals. There has been many a hero in this war, who without a thought, much less a regret, has given his life for a comrade whom he has seen lying wounded. I had to quarrel with my men about it constantly. On active service often you have to upbraid when in secret you applaud. A combatant soldier in full fighting health should not risk his life for a man no longer fit. To do so is better saint-ship than warfare. It's poor warfare. But Tommy does it all the time. He hangs over a wounded fellow as a mother hangs over an ailing baby. Let that same fellow be killed, and Tommy will call him 'that 'ere bloomin' stiff un', move him a bit out of his own way with his foot, and brew cocoa in the lee of the corpse. Tommy has his complexities.

The devotion of the men to their officers is throat-choking. With two *possible* exceptions – the devotion of native soldiers to their British officers in Indian regiments, and the devotion of the black slave soldiers to their white master officers in the Confederate Army in the American Civil War – I doubt if history can equal the present war's example of such fine-spirited loyalty. I know of a case where for two days and nights an officer's servant lay beside his wounded master, shielding him with his own body; and when that living shield seemed to be getting inadequate, the man buried the now unconscious officer, and kept small air-holes open with his own careful fingers. He lost one finger as he worked at this amateur supplying of oxygen – but he worked on. He was pinked in the shoulder – but he worked on. And he saved the life for which he so persistently risked his own. Gallipoli teemed with such acts of loyalty. No, I do not think we shall find, when the holocaust is over, that this war has blunted or cheapened the finer instincts of men simply or highly born. It seems to me that a higher Power steps in, when man's nerve otherwise must reach its breaking-point, and dulls for the time being only, but does not allow to be destroyed, some of the natural sensitiveness which we call 'finer', or gives to soldiers on active service a superhuman control of its expression. If it were not so, there could be no fighting; it would be impossible to carry on.

The next day I had to go down with the artillery observation officer to a position on our right. My business there was as prosaic and uninteresting as it was necessary. But I remember getting an amusing side-light on the character of one type of British combatant.

'Do you see that chap?' my companion said – we were in his position now – pointing out a figure squatting over a bubbling kettle.

I did see him. He was very visible. A London cockney, if ever one wore khaki; a gunner, red-faced, pugnacious in a discreet way, at once shrewd, and dense, of uncertain age, munching bully-beef and smoking a rank pipe at the same time.

'I was rather short of sentries last night, and I had to put him on. He hadn't done that work before. I noticed him by-and-by walking up and down in rather a jerky way, and occasionally bobbing down to the ground. There were a few shells just then going over his head into that little wood over there. I went up to him, and he sprang up mighty stern and straight, and we went through the usual formula of "Halt! Who goes there?" etc. "All right, sir," he said in the chummiest way when the formalities were disposed of. "Beg pardon, sir; didn't recognise you."

'How the devil could he with his nose in the ground? But I ignored that, and said, "Well, Jones, how are you getting on?"

'"Not very nice, sir. Them shells are a bit near, an' I've got a missus an' seven kids at 'ome in Lunnon, sir" —

'"Yes, yes, Jones," I said hastily, but as soothingly as I could; "but they aren't shelling you – they are shelling the wood. Good-night, Jones."

'But Jones wasn't done with me yet. "Beggin' your pardon, sir, but 'ow far are the henemy's trenches?"

"'Oh, let me see – about two hundred yards away, I think."

"'Thank you, sir. An' 'ow far are hour reserve-trenches away, sir?"

"'Um," I told him – "oh, about eight hundred yards, I should say."

'Jones was a man again! "Thank you, sir," he said heartily. "Good-night, an' good luck, sir. There is no Turk can give me two 'undred yards in a thousand!"'

On coming back 'home' up the trench I met a stretcher coming down. An orderly who was walking in front told me it held Captain M'Lagan, the Acting C.O., who had been hit in the leg by a sniper. He was quite cheery, and assured me he would be back soon. I met him a long time afterwards in Edinburgh, and he told me that all I had said to him was 'Damn you!' – only that, in an angry tone – and had passed on indignantly. And probably it was true. I don't think I had felt sympathetic in the least. He could ill be spared. There never was a better leader. And we needed our best at the Dardanelles. He was every inch a soldier, as full as he could be of pluck and resourcefulness. He received the D.S.O. in the second award of honours.

I saw red when I learned he was out of it even temporarily. We simply could not spare him, and for myself I was bitterly annoyed, because this made me O.C. Battalion, and that was just the last thing I wanted. I had quite enough to do, and more than enough to 'carry' without any additional responsibility. I am no more superior to ambition than other men are. To say that I have ever had an advance in rank without being greatly pleased would be ridiculous, and it would be grossly untrue. But my nerves were on edge just then, I was working under terrible pressure, and the constant crisis at Gallipoli was such that an older and far better soldier than I might, in sheer patriotism, have shrunk from unaccustomed authority, from new and terrible responsibilities. I loathed it at the time. Looked back at, it is a different matter, and, frankly, it is the one thing in life of which I am intensely proud, and I feel about it very much as Leigh Hunt felt about having been kissed by Mrs Carlyle.

> Time, you thief! who live to get
> Sweets into your list, put that in.
> Say I'm weary, say I'm sad;
> Say that health and wealth have missed me;
> Say I'm growing old, but add –

that I commanded my own battalion in the field, a battalion of the 29th Division. It was only for eight days, and we gained over two hundred yards.

Having received orders that more progress must be made, I decided to advance the next evening after dark. There was only one captain left now (Captain Macrae), so I gave him the job, telling him to be particularly careful of himself, and that he should have support if he found he needed it.

They crept forward, and everything seemed to be going all right, when suddenly men came tumbling into the trench, crying out that they had received orders to retreat. I can't say which was greater, my consternation or my fury. What a beginning!

In a case like this you must make up your mind quickly. I chanced to have a Very light pistol in my hand. I clapped it to the head of the nearest man beside me, and told him I'd shoot him dead if he didn't go over the top at once; and I meant it.

It was a touch-and-go moment. The men were unnerved. But we won through. I was greatly helped by a lance-corporal who gathered a few of them together and made them follow him. I have wondered often and often who he was, but have never managed to trace him. He would have been recommended if I could have learned his name.

My pistol had the desired effect, and they all, unmanned for but a moment, scurried off as pell-mell and as fast as they'd come, and went over the top again like true Britons. I went too, to have a look around. It was all quite quiet!

If I could have found the individual who had given the order – for I think that some one had – there would have been a whole heap of trouble for him; but I could fix the blame on no one. Fortunately it was only a section that had got jumpy. The rest, on the right, where the officer was, were perfectly in hand.

We managed to go on for two hundred yards and a little more, and our casualties were astonishingly slight.

The next morning we came in for a particularly bad time. We were enfiladed from an enemy trench on our left. After a bit of hard work we got a barricade built, and it was a material help. But we had lost one of our best sergeants, and in the afternoon we had the cruel bad luck to lose one of our subalterns, Lieutenant Kemp – an invaluable boy. A sniper got him. Moreover, we had loved him, and his death, and the hard way we saw him die, cast gloom over us all. We were down now to two captains (including myself) and two subalterns (Lieutenants Maule and Murdoch), and the outlook was not rosy. The continual losing of officers depresses men badly. However, we had to carry on, and we did; each one did his bit. ·

Every morning promptly at four the Turkish fusillade began, and it rarely ceased or slacked while the enemy could see to aim. They aimed well. But nothing out of the ordinary happened for a day or two. One evening a chit came through from headquarters: General Williams presented his compliments, and desired me to breakfast with him the next morning.

I had to rise at three to get myself titivated to look as presentable as was possible. Primping is difficult in the trenches. I had to start off at half-past four at the very latest. It wasn't healthy near here after that. So, soon after four, my orderly and I sallied forth. We arrived at headquarters safely. I had to wait about until eight. But I had a good rest while I waited, and amused myself reading antique newspapers.

One by one the other C.O.s arrived. With military promptitude, we breakfasted on time to the second. I had imagined somehow that the breakfast would be better than I had had for a long time. It was not. I cannot accuse the staff of doing themselves at all well. I really think that I did myself better at my own mess.

One of the staff from the headquarters boat came in after breakfast, and we all went off to have a walk around the entire position. Going by the Gurkha Bluff, we got on the high ground on the extreme left, and had a fine view of the position. It was three in the afternoon before we got back. At the end of our jaunt we had a great sprint across a field. A sniper or some snipers had spotted us, and we had to run for all we were worth. And we did, including the general.

I was very hungry when we got into headquarters, and I fully expected a nice lunch. But there was nothing doing. A cup of tea and a bit of cake from some one's parcel was all the provender we saw. Then we settled down to a long official pow-wow. While we were talking a gaunt figure appeared in the entrance to the dug-out. To my astonishment, it was my own colonel. He had recovered, or thought he had, from his wounds, and was reporting for duty. The general wished him to go back to the beach, at least for the night, but he insisted that he must stay and consult with me. The general shook his head, but said, 'Oh well, then, if you must, I suppose you must. Wait till I've finished with Mure, then.'

After the confab I rejoined my C.O., and found him determined to come up to the firing-line with me, and then go back to the beach. He looked so ill that I'd have ordered him back to hospital then and there if I had had the authority. But I could not order my superior officer; it is not done in the army. The officer commanding the Engineers of the 29th Division was coming up with me, so we three started off together. All went well till we got to Clapham Junction (half Gallipoli had British names by now), when a bullet went whiz between my legs. In a moment another shaved the colonel a shade closer. We thought it wise to take cover. We did; but after we'd waited a minute or two, I did my usual sprint of fifty yards or so to see if the sniper would have another go. But he made no sign, so I took fresh cover, and then waved to the others to come on, one at a time. They got across all right. We were now in a dip, and soon got very near the firing-line. There was an open bit here which was almost always under fire; you could not go into it by daylight without calling forth a shower of fire; yet, very oddly, only two men were hit crossing it all the twelve days we were there. We three did another sprint through it, and got safely home.

Every one was pleased to see our C.O., and he seemed pleased to be with us again; and he stayed so long that it would have been dark long before he could have got back to the beach. So he stayed all night; in fact, he didn't go back at all. It was awfully plucky of him, coming back so soon. He couldn't move his arm more than about six inches, and had to be helped on with his coat. I was very sorry for him that night. He was tall. The only place I could put him was a cursed little hole dug into the face of the trench. He had to curl into it like a dog, and with his sore arm that couldn't have been much fun. I passed him several times during the night, and I don't think he slept once; but he never complained.

We had a jumpy time that night. We had to stand-to several times. And one of Bairnsfather's famous pictures, in which Adjutant B. has been called to the 'phone in the midst of action to be asked how many tins of plum and apple had been received yesterday, reminds me of a little incident of my own that same night. About half-past twelve I lay down to get a rest. In a quarter of an hour I was roused to answer the 'phone. This entailed a walk of at least two hundred yards along the trench and over sleeping men all the way. It was the signal officer who wished to speak to me at the other end of the wire. He informed me that in future no parties were to be allowed to proceed to the beach to bathe without being accompanied by an officer. I informed him that he was an unhappy blend of blooming ass and blithering idiot. We knew each other well personally, and I added other unprintable language. Really, it was adding insult to injury, as my battalion had never had a chance to have a sea-bathe since we had landed a month ago. And at one in the morning!

We had done twelve days now up in this blasted wood, and we were pleased the next morning when orders came that we were to be relieved. I didn't go down myself with the advance party, but sent a subaltern with it to the rest-camp which headquarters said was all prepared for us.

We left Fir-Tree Wood early the next morning. We went off casually by platoons, not to attract attention, and to let the Turks think it was just the usual ration-parties and such. For, unless there was a strafe on, they didn't bother these parties much.

If an unbroken daisy-field is a prepared rest-camp under the Act – well then, I apologise.

Chapter 16

The Pink Farm

It was still early in the morning when we had all arrived at a tumble-down building, covered with a faded red roof (or what once had been a roof), and rejoicing in the name of the Pink Farm. We were to camp about fifty yards to the right of the ruined house. We started at once to dig ourselves in, and to make ourselves in that and other ways as comfortable as British troops might hope to be in Gallipoli. The Turks were not quite always with us, but the useful spade was.

We had been in the peninsula a month now, and on our second day at the Pink Farm our first draft arrived from home. We were jolly glad to see them. There were two officers with them, who had been sergeants with the old regiment at mobilisation. The men had been recruited mainly from Bo'ness, and were miners by trade. As they should take naturally to digging, I immediately commandeered them to dig an officers' mess, and in a couple of days we had a splendid dug-out just in front of the old farmhouse. I had managed to abstract from the beach some wood, wire netting, and sandbags. These made a capital roof; so at last we had a little comfort. We had earned it.

Then thirteen officers rolled up, fresh from home and Kitchener's Army. They were keener than mustard, and did great work. Two of them got the Military Cross before long. It was wonderful how the reinforcement brightened us all. We had needed it so! We had not had the advantage of the prescribed 10 per cent over strength to make good first casualties.

We decided to have a bathe, as a very unique sort of house-warming, and parties were detailed to go off by relays. The first party went off under the C.O., and promptly the shells of the Turk began to dance hot attendance.

Lieutenant Maule – our second-last original subaltern – was standing beside me when the mischief began. He ran down at once to tell the men to get into their dug-outs – sometimes they would not go unless they were ordered – when bang came a shell into the midst of the party. I lost sight of my subaltern in the dust of earth and shell. I was straining my eyes to find him, when word was brought to me that he was killed. It was not yet four minutes since he had left me. For a moment it seemed to me as if— Oh, well! I had loved the lad.

He had just reached the men, when a shell pounded down, and a piece of it pierced through his lungs and his heart. Except a man who was grazed on the arm, no one else got a scratch.

I ran down to the boy, and I could almost think he was sleeping; he looked so quiet and peaceful. There was a smile on his face. And I wished that his 'people' could see him.

I never had felt anything as I felt that subaltern's death. I had trained him myself. A more unselfish fellow didn't exist. He always thought of himself last. He was more than popular with the men. I saw several of them crying, and I felt like it myself. He had been given a 'cushy' job on the G.H.Q. boat, but pleaded to get back to the battalion.

And he was the brawest gentleman
That was amang them a'.

We buried many an officer of ours at the Dardanelles, but being in rest, we buried him best and gentlest of all. That was all we could do for him. And we did it.

At dusk I laid him in his grave at the foot of a tree, near the grave of one of his own men who had been killed that day, and I put posts and a shielding fence of barbed wire around it all. It is there now, I make no doubt, unless some stray last shell went that way, or a Hun came down after we'd gone – for I believe the Turk respects such sanctuary.

We were hid by the farm. Shells might find us, but field–glasses could not. So we held a service at his open grave, and as many were there as I would allow, as many as could be assembled with safety – and a few more.

Some of those rough men sobbed frankly. The padre himself nearly broke down, very, very used as he was to such ceremonies. I turned and walked away. I was glad of the dark. The tears were running down my face.

A storm was coming up. The Aegean curled and moaned, and the guns of the Turk thundered a dirge. And a boy lay dead two thousand miles from home, buried by stealth in alien earth.

However, one must just carry on. So in the morning I determined to have a bathe and a bit of a holiday. My valise had turned up, and at last I could manage a change of raiment. I required it, too. My minute visitors were exercising 'squatter sovereignty' on me with a vengeance, having taken up their abode round my middle in increasing numbers. And they throve on me, and increased as if they'd been Shylock's ducats or Australian rabbits.

I shall never forget that bathe. The water was lukewarm. It looked like green fire with the sun full on it. You could sit in it up to your neck, keeping your helmet on for protection. I wanted to throw away my old undergarments, but the C.O., who had come with me, wouldn't hear of this. He ordered me to tie a big stone to them, and put them where they would be washed by the sea, but would not float away. And then I could get them the next time I came down. I meekly did as I was told, but I vowed to myself that I never would look for the blasted lousy things – and I never did.

I began my holiday the following morning. I longed to get away from everyone and everything, especially returns. So I got permission, borrowed a horse, and off I went, free and alone for one blessed day. I went carefully attired. I rather fancied my own appearance – as much of it as I could see. I discarded my Tommy's uniform, and sneaked a pair of transport-driver's breeches. They fitted me almost too well – so well that I couldn't take them off myself at night. I put on my own officer's coat, and with a khaki handkerchief made up as a hunting-scarf, gaily set off, feeling an awful 'nut'. I risked the sun and wore my glengarry, and that made me a Jock. And on that peninsula, then, a Jock was a very important person. And my badge showed that I belonged to No. 1 Regiment of Foot in the British Army.

No holiday could have been more simple. But, oh, how I enjoyed it! A whole day with not a duty in it! I could scarcely believe that I was I, and much less that I was in Gallipoli.

I cantered over the ridge behind our position, to get out of any possible harm as quickly as possible, and then I trotted across to begin my day with a bathe. It was incredible how changed the place was. I came across a farrier busily shoeing horses just as if this were the British country-side he'd grown up in. The last time I had been near the spot it had been decidedly unpleasant. I found a man to hold my cuddy, and I had a topping bathe. Then I rode off again along the cliff to have a look at X Beach, which I had never seen. This part of the peninsula is lovely. I shouldn't be at all surprised to hear that a syndicate had started to lay out golf-courses and build a casino there. It's an ideal place for a syndicate of capitalists to spoil.

I arrived at X Beach – and I held my breath. How men landed there at all must always be a mystery to me. A fly could hardly hang on to the place.

I went on to W Beach. And again I was astonished to see the vast deal that had been done. A road had been made at the foot of the cliff; terraces of dug-outs had been constructed on the slopes. (We didn't stay in Gallipoli very long, but, by Jove! we honeycombed it while we did stay.) And everywhere was a hive of industry. I felt quite lost, a stranger in a strange place, 'all dressed up, and nowhere to go', and for a disappointed moment my holiday was threatened by a feeling of strain. I had a hunt round, but could find no one I'd ever seen before. I was hungry, so I went to the old whereabouts of our quartermaster's department. It had gone, and no one seemed to know whither it had been moved. But I found it at last – and lunch. In looking out to sea I noticed, close inshore, part of a vessel sticking out of the water. It was all that was left of the *Majestic*. She turned turtle when she was torpedoed. One of her crew – a loyal soul, I suppose, and certainly a very cool one, and quite the last to leave her – had stuck on as she heeled over. He ran along the ram – it just showed above the water – undressed leisurely, made his garments into a neat bundle, put it on his head, jumped into the sea, and slowly swam ashore, to the wild applause of many ecstatic Tommies.

As the sun was sinking I saddled Peggy, and she and I had a splendid ride home in the cool of the evening.

I found everything quite normal, ate my dinner, signed the usual returns, digested a *Weekly Scotsman* I'd got hold of, and went off to bed.

I always look back on that day as the best holiday I ever had. It was the only break I had in six seething, scorching weeks. After enough excitement to last any reasonable creature a lifetime, the tensest of all possible excitements, with the continual probability of being shot the next second thrown in for emotional make-weight, one is calculated to appreciate a little change, and to find in the mildest of holiday-making some smack of paradise.

I spent the next day making plans and getting bearings of all our graves. Headquarters wanted them. Fortunately I already had most of them, or I could never have finished the list in time.

There was one thing that pleased me. I found that his broken pipes, which I had placed on the poor piper's grave over a month ago, were still there. I wonder if they are there yet. I hope so.

Chapter 17

Is It Written?

The fulfilled premonitions of war-time are enormous in number and quite indisputable in fact. The proportion of fulfilments that I have known personally inclines me to think that premonition has more significance than chance. On the other hand, unfulfilled premonitions are far from rare among soldiers, as it is only fair to admit.

But one striking difference I have noted between premonitions fulfilled and justified and those unfulfilled and discredited is that the former were usually dated and fairly definite in detail, whereas the latter were almost always vague and pointed to no date. The fulfilled were to the unfulfilled in the ratio of about five to one.

I expected my turn of the bullet or the shell to come in Gallipoli – but it never did. I expected it rather in a spirit of *esprit de corps*, I think, than in the spirit of prophecy. I expected, rather than felt, that it would come. And I never felt that I should be killed. One day an orderly, who was somewhat long in doing an errand, showed me his helmet when he came back, with a bullet-hole through its side, and the ventilator in the top knocked off. He remarked to me, 'I'm all right, sir. They won't kill me.' Poor boy, he got his head taken right off by a shell a week later.

The long-range, half-spent bullet had an extraordinary way of getting men. The day before we left the Pink Farm one of my orderlies who had been with me the whole time, going to and fro between Brigade Headquarters and our own several times a day, and often under heavy fire, was sitting on the side of my dug-out reading the *Weekly Scotsman* while waiting for some message from me. Before I could finish writing it I had to go to the quartermaster's stores. Everything was peculiarly quiet. I never heard a bullet either going or coming. On getting back I noticed that my orderly was no longer there, but I thought nothing of it. He'd be back in a moment. He was not far off. I finished my message and shouted for him. Another man answered my call. The orderly had been wounded, and the stretcher-bearers had taken him away already.

Yes, really, I am inclined to believe what most old soldiers believe. They are fatalists, most of them, and say that the bullet with their name on its label will get them, no matter where they are. For instance, a man went through our first five weeks of Gallipoli as a runner, running under the most dangerous conditions. With no communication-trenches to walk in, he had to cross open spaces under constant and concentrated fire. The Turks must often have known he was a messenger. Yet he escaped unscathed. And then, when one might have imagined he was quite safe, he got knocked out. I saw him not long ago – as an officer – and he still carries that Turkish bullet inside him.

Again, one day at the Pink Farm I wished to go to the stores dump. I happened to be in our officers' mess dug-out. It was also my orderly-room – our Gallipolian housekeeping was the acme of concentration. It was open at both ends. I left at the end least convenient for my errand, a form of stupidity, I think, not quite characteristic. I wondered why I had done so, and before I had gone five yards a shell landed plump at the other entrance. The earth and the stones it threw up landed about me. Had I used the more convenient exit, I must have been killed. Coming back I made a slight detour to speak to a sergeant, and – I couldn't possibly have said why – again entered the mess by the less convenient hole of the two – this time the entrance opposite that which I had used on going to the dump. As I passed in a second shell fell and exploded at the end I had gone out by, and once more earth and stones spattered about me. Twice in less than a quarter of an hour my life had been saved by my own quite inadvertent blunder. Coincidence merely? H'm – perhaps! I don't quite know what I think about it. Of course, it may have been the merest chance – but still it is undeniably curious.

We were a ragged lot when we tramped down to the Pink Farm. While we were there a ship came in. It brought all manner of needed things, and we managed to get quite a supply of clothing. The garments were various, and the parts of a suit did not always match, nor did the supply altogether go round, but the men whose clothes were in the worst condition all managed to get new things.

This reminds me of an interesting correspondence on the habits of the louse. At least, I thought it very interesting at the time, and it gives a fair idea of the great time and trouble our army takes over minute detail. Certainly, if Carlyle's definition of genius, 'the transcendent capacity of taking trouble, first of all,' is correct, our War Office must be the temple of genius.

A unit felt aggrieved because of the part-worn clothing that was being reissued to it, so the adjutant took the matter up with the staff officer responsible for the issue. Part (only part, please notice) of Minute 1 – official *billets-doux* are always called 'minutes' in the army – stated that 'several of the kilts received have been found to contain a large number of lice eggs. Most of these eggs are possibly dead, but according to the habits of lice it is probable that some of them are still fertile, which might mean the infection of the whole battalion.'

The reply in Minute 2 stated: 'With reference to the lice eggs mentioned by you, by a special process these are thoroughly sterilised by the cleaners here, the process and the results being to the satisfaction of the local medical authorities. No possible danger rests therein, and the dead eggs could only be removed to the detriment of the kilt. Finally, in connection with the habits of lice mentioned in your letter, the views stated therein are erroneous. The eggs of the lice (*Pediculus vestimenti*) germinate after nine or ten days or die (A. E. Shipley, Sc.D., Christ's College, Cambridge). They further depend entirely upon the body for their existence, and quickly die apart from it. They cannot live for any length of time in discarded clothing. In this respect they differ profoundly from the bug and the flea, which may be considered as only occasionally living upon the body (B. E. Cummings, Department of Entomology, British Museum).'

This evidently was a stumper for our friend the adjutant, because all he could raise in his reply in Minute 3 was that 'your information regarding the habits of lice, fleas, and bugs is most interesting, and may be considered satisfactory.'

Just such trouble is taken over any subject that crops up – even in all the stress of active service. And yet there are people who say that only the Germans are thorough.

At the front the stores and the dumps are rather like a broker's shop. The army deals in anything from needles and pins to ore by the ton.

I do not know the end of the above correspondence, but let us hope that the *Pediculus vestimenti* in the kilt was 'kilt entirely' before the new wearer assumed the garb of old Gaul.

Chapter 18

The Battle of Krithia

We had been at the Pink Farm not quite five days, when orders came at half-past six in the afternoon that the battalion would move to the firing-line that night at eight via the Gurkha Bluff, the large, deep nullah that was rendered famous by the Indian Highlanders.

If every fight I saw in Gallipoli defies and baffles all description, the thrice-bloody battle of Krithia beggars every other. It was hell heaped up, running over, multiplied a thousandfold. We went through it only, I think, because the intensest human sense of suffering and sensibility to torture are reached in a *comparatively* mild stage of battle. Men suffer all they can suffer in battles many times less ardent, less concentrated of agony, than was Krithia. And when men have reached their acme of pain and of horror, the piling up of more does not affect their sense of woe, even if it be heaped higher than 'old Pelion, or the skyish head of blue Olympus'.

Modern war is a mosaic of tiny fragments, cemented together by human blood, hammered together by ten thousand individual energies. Each man does his bit. Few men see or know much of the whole. Only a soldier of the Higher Command could have known much at the time of our war at the Dardanelles. I was a very small piece in that hideous mosaic. Even of the battle of Krithia, though I was in it for two days and nights, I saw but my own minute part. I could describe comprehensively the Dardanelles campaign, or Krithia, only by borrowing from reports that for the most part are as accessible to all as they are to me. Incomparably more competent pens can do that bigger task. I think it more useful to attempt a plain, unvarnished record of what I saw and of what I tried to help to do.

We left the rest-camp precisely at eight, and as we crested the rise the nightly fusillade began, and almost at once the bullets were spitting about and among us, not single spies, but whole battalions.

It was my third spell of going up, through fire, to the front line, and I began to feel the continued strain.

Only two of us – the original officers – had not been touched up to now. And I admit that I was beginning to imagine that my turn must be coming soon. Partly this was nerves; a little, I fancy, it was mathematical; and to some extent it came from seeing the casualties we had before getting into the Gurkha Bluff. One fellow got it when he was just beside me, and it made me feel jumpy – a sensation I had not had before. However, there was nothing for it but to carry on, and we plodded and scrambled on to the point where we went up the cliff into the support-trenches. I certainly felt 'fey' that night. I am not boasting of my second-sight, for it proved entirely false, unless the feeling merely presaged break-down. My first wound has not found me yet, and my sleeve has no right to wear the little strip of gold which the boys coveted, and which we older men as ardently hoped to escape.

We had been just an hour and a half grilling through the bullets and the dark when we were abruptly halted by a sudden block in front of us. We could not wedge into it, try as we would, so the men lay down. There we stayed until after one, when the block gave way a bit, and we succeeded in pushing past the Indian Brigade, and moving up till we reached our sector. By the time we had settled down it was feeding-time, but there were no mess orderlies on view – and so, no breakfast.

Orders came in the morning that the regiment would remain in their trench, and hold it at all cost, if the attacking troops (who would arrive an hour before their time for advancing to the attack) were forced back.

Whether or not this would be pleasanter for us than advancing ourselves remained to be seen.

I established my 'phone at about the centre of the position, and then I arranged the companies.

This was the programme: There was to be bombardment for three-quarters of an hour. Then the men were to show their bayonets over the top and cheer. Then – another bombardment for fifteen minutes, and over you go!

Armoured cars were to be used for the first time, and the Royal Engineers were putting planks of wood over our trenches so that the cars could go across that way. There was a flagman to show the driver the way, and where the place was. But the flagman didn't waggle his flag properly, and that led to my undoing.

Besides keeping communication up in my own unit, we had orders to render an hourly report on the battle, which meant a lot of running about and interrogating the wounded as they came back. For even the wounded must help, if they can, and they are always eager to do so.

The programme began at the scheduled moment. It was the stiffest time I had seen since the hideous struggle of the first landing. After a short while it got too warm even for Anzacs and Twenty-ninthers, not from the fire of the foe, but from the well-meant (if not well-aimed) guns of our own navy. Their heavies began to fall perilously near our trench; and when one landed just behind it, I got on the 'phone and harangued headquarters earnestly. And the range of the navy's guns soon increased.

I am trying to tell, from the personal point of view, a little of what the 29th Division of our army did in Gallipoli; but it should always be borne in mind that the Dardanelles campaign was a naval enterprise, and that we were there for a sub-navy purpose: to assist our ships to force a passage through the straits, and to win the enormous all that that would entail and secure. It was a naval venture, and in the battle of Krithia, as in all the engagements, our ships were of constant and great assistance. We were fighting their battle; naturally they threw their might in with ours.

The bombardment ceased as sharply as it had begun. The men rattled their bayonets and cheered. A yell for victory and for home went up from every throat there. Then the second spasm commenced. It was fast. It was furious. Words pale before it. Memory sickens at it.

It stopped, and up over the top went the first line. Evidently the Turk had been lying low, for now his machine-guns grew very active; and a terrible stream of wounded came flowing back to us.

But now the supports came pouring through us like good wine – or liquid iron – through tired veins. That steadied things up a bit. An armoured car came with them, spitting and puffing and lumbering along. Nothing so ugly or so awkward ever was seen outside of a Zoo. The very amateur bridge that the Engineers had tossed up for them was just beside my 'phone. The flagman waved a bit of rag about three inches square, and the car made for it. She got on to the planks all right; *then!* – her off hind-wheel slipped over the side, and down she came on to the axle, and (incidentally) pretty well on to my head. Nothing could be done, so the naval officer in charge and the gunner climbed out. In getting out the naval petty officer was seriously wounded.

The attack was not progressing quite up to time, but we were getting on in patches.

Unfortunately the Turks were getting on in patches too. At this point my position was about four hundred yards from a nasty-looking trench of the enemy's, and they soon spotted our broken-down car.

Then the fun began. A battery started to try to blow the car to blazes. They made a good start. What with this and machine-gun bullets jumping off the car at all angles, I was having a thin time. I cannot recall ever having had a thinner. To add to my trouble, my wire was in too constant requisition. It was the only one working, and officers from other units were finding me out and wanting to use it every few minutes.

I had just written out two messages and given them to two orderlies. I felt restless, and got up, turned about aimlessly, and moved away some ten yards. That restlessness saved my life. At that moment a shell crashed into the trench and exploded precisely where I had been sitting. Frankly, it made me feel peculiar. I remember that I stumbled a bit as I walked on, thinking that if I had stayed where I was, or gone the other way, I should, by now, have been blown to little bits. I finished what I wanted to do (for my aimlessness had been but an instant's – we had no time for aimlessness then) – and went back to the trench. I met one of my orderlies, who, fortunately for him, had left immediately with the first message I had written. He had bits of shrapnel in his jaw, in his elbow, and in his back. I bound him up and packed him off. I got back into the trench, and saw what I had not seen before, for the smoke had cleared now. My other orderly lay dead, with my message still in his hand. His body and his head lay four or five feet apart. Two of my signallers were killed also, and mutilated so horribly that to describe their condition would be inexcusable. I stood for a moment and gazed at the wreckage – wreck of trench, wreck of 'phone, wreck of men, and then I sat dully down on the mud floor of the trench.

Chapter 19

All In!

But, of course, I had to stick it out, so I rose and got my report off through the battered 'phone, which the surviving signallers just managed to make work once more, by propping it here, splicing it there.

I was now infernally hungry – it was well on in the afternoon – but there was no sign of food. So I had a look at the beastly car, which was still there – I dare say it is there now – and in it I found bully-beef and biscuits. Bully-beef is not my special weakness, but I ate that bully-beef for all it was worth, and I always have liked biscuits.

In one of the attacks that day a small party of an English regiment rushed a machine-gun, and succeeded in capturing it and the officer in charge, who was only slightly wounded. It happened to be a volunteer crew who manned the gun, a crew from the *Goeben*, which was so much in evidence early in the war. The officer in command of the machine-gun was a Prussian. He was wild at being captured. He commanded (and then he begged) to be shot dead rather than be taken prisoner. 'No, sir,' an English Tommy told him; 'we are British soldiers, not Germans.' Tommy has his feelings, but he also has his failings. His feelings are nasty ones at times, and at times his tongue is nasty too. I saw that Hun officer ten minutes after he was captured. He had the typical Prussian face.

The C.O., who had been going up and down the line all the time, came in while I was still munching my stolen biscuits, and we had a serious confab, and together we contrived to get a fairly extensive report off to headquarters. The battle had practically ceased now. I am afraid that in the centre of the position where we were not much progress had been made. In fact, I learned long afterwards that I had been practically as far as we ever got in that particular bit of the line. The C.O. told me that I would get some dinner if I went down to the gully, and he kindly waited till I came back.

I went to the gully, and I got some dinner; but I felt that there was something very wrong with me. I couldn't quite diagnose what it was. My spine seemed to be misplaced, and to be made of glue rather than of bone; yet I could walk all right. I went back at about half-past seven, and started my usual evening's work. But I was listless. I could neither rest nor really work. Nothing interested me – nothing! At half-past two I gave it up and lay down, but I couldn't sleep. What I did from four till about half-past seven I have never been able to remember. Perhaps I shall some day, but I fancy not. I believe that those three or four hours of my life are dead, and for ever buried in the chalky loam of Gallipoli. At half-past seven I struggled down to the gully for breakfast. It was torture to walk. It was torture to think. It was double torture to be.

I remember chatting quite cheerfully with some one, I cannot recall with whom, as I began to eat, and then something suddenly snapped, and I collapsed into a sort of maudlin, weeping condition. I was all in.

I felt that I was going silly, and that I *must* have a rest, if only for one day. I had been under fire for forty-two days. And during all that time I had had very little sleep, barely tasting it now and then, just enough of it to whet to stronger agony my appetite and need for it.

I did not require to tell the C.O. when I got back – how I did get back I do not remember; he saw at once what a plight I was in, and he packed me off immediately for three days' leave. And he gave me a note to the medical officer at the beach. I pulled myself together enough to arrange a few matters that I ought not to leave at loose ends, got my bag, and went off by myself, not wishing to see or speak to any one.

And even now I'd rather not write of the little I remember of how I got to the beach. It was mine, my very own, and I'll keep it so. I roamed and groped about forlornly. I was dazed, and for the most part my memory had forsaken me. I remember laughing once or twice when I heard the guns go, pleased as a child. And why not? I was a child again, a stray child, alone in Gallipoli.

My mind rebalanced itself partly after a time, but not my body. I hunted for the M.O. to whom the commanding officer had given me a chit; but I could not find him, and presently I lay down on my back, feeling absolutely helpless, and wondering peevishly if he'd find me. For two hours or more I never moved. Then I crawled back to the hospital tent. I crawled in and held out my note. An officer took it – not he to whom it was addressed – and, after a sharp glance at me, opened and read it. He directed me to another marquee. It was near enough, and I found it and lurched in. I was swaying now like a man very drunk. An officer got up quickly, and looked at me hard. I held out my note again. The officer in the other tent had written something on the envelope, but I had no curiosity as to what it was, and I hadn't glanced at it. And I believe that I could not have read then, not even very big print.

This officer never spoke, but just looked at me, wrote something on a ticket, and pinned it on my coat. Then he said regretfully that the place was full up – choked – and that I'd better rest about a bit, and come back at seven in the morning, and that then I'd be put on board a ship. I heard what he said, but it did not mean much to me. He had to tell me a second or a third time to go away until the next day, and then I did stagger out and off again. I remember distinctly that my feelings were hurt. I wanted a home. I desired to be coddled. And I was turned out, and very homeless.

I meandered about for a while, and by luck I tumbled across the acting quartermaster. He took me to his dug-out, and a glass of rum steadied me a bit. We sat and talked for a long time; at least, he talked, and supplied me with rum *ad. lib.* Curiously enough – for I was very weak, and had scarcely eaten for I don't know how long – it had not the least effect on me. Finally I lay down, and I dozed off and on until about five; and then I had some breakfast, and wandered back to the hospital tent. There I found the last officer left of one of the original regiments. He had a bullet in his leg, and we walked down to the pier together, leaning on each other.

Walking none too steadily across the pontoon pier (and little thinking that it was my passing from Gallipoli), I had a narrow squeak. The pier was crowded. Half of it was covered with stretcher cases. We were half-way across when a hideous scream came hurtling through the air. I exclaimed involuntarily, 'My God, we're in for it!' when splash into the water beside us went a great shell. Its spray drenched us, and spattered the wounded, and some of them began to groan.

They were working on the beach that day as I had never seen men work before. Like Trojans? No; like Britons and Twenty-ninthers. I don't believe the Trojan wars, fought so near here, ever saw such herculean labour so herculeanly performed. Even the 'brass hats' had thrown off their coats, and were carrying stretchers. It was a great campaign, and great men fought it.

I went to the end of the pier and sat down, absolutely not caring one minute what became of me, and the next minute praying to God for a boat to take me off the awful place. And when you pray at the front, you pray fervently. No slack prayers go up from the firing-line! By this time I had lost the officer with whom I had limped down, and was quite alone. I met him again on the ship at Lemnos.

I was in a dirty mood now. I would do nothing for any one. How long I sat on the pier I have no idea, but eventually I found myself on a pinnace. I don't remember how I got there, but probably the midshipman in charge had carried me. He was not half my size, or nearly half my age; but he was a dominant person. We scudded out to sea, and soon we came alongside a tug-boat. I boarded her willingly enough, and some one showed me my way down to a tiny cabin.

I sat down. And then it dawned on me that I actually was sitting on a cushioned seat. I laughed. Nearly, I wanted to cry. And for the moment I scarcely could believe it. I was on a cushion! A carpet under my feet! I was not in a trench! And where were the smells and the dead and the bullets? I actually was not in a trench! When I had grown just a little used to that stupendous fact, I looked feebly about me. There was a sideboard opposite me. There were bottles on it – lots of bottles. I kept my eye on them, and when a steward came in I asked him for a drink. He went away, and brought me a cup of tea. I told him to take his tea somewhere, and bring me something stronger. He replied that he was not allowed to do that, as the bottles were solely for the use of the ship's officers. Evidently it was no use arguing. I had been up against ship's rules and skipper discipline before, so I meekly took the tea.

I felt the boat moving. Dulled and half-dead as my senses were, my emotions were indescribable. My blood leapt in my tired veins, exultant that I had left Gallipoli; but my heart clove to the battalion – the tattered, battered remains of it, fighting and festering in the trenches, on the beach, across the nullahs. I felt a deserter.

And a lot of use I'd have been – if I could have gone back! I only just managed to get upstairs when they sent for me, only just managed with the assistance of my inexorable he-Hebe of the tea-pot. We were in Lemnos harbour, and lying close beside the *Southland*; the last time I had seen her I had been embarking from a port in England. Directed to do so, I went up the companion-way, and found myself on a magnificent vessel, absolutely packed with wounded.

I was pushed along to a doctor who was taking names and issuing brisk orders. I told him that he need not bother about my name, as I must get off at once, for I had only three days' leave, and feared it was nearly up. He smiled curtly, and informed me that I was not getting off until I got off at Alexandria. I began to expostulate. I was wretchedly upset. I insisted that there was nothing wrong with me, and that I must and would get off. He turned kind at that, and told me not to be ashamed of being a very ill man; that I was chewed up, body and soul; and that my cabin was 412. I really wasn't able to argue, so I went off to the cabin, and threw myself on my bunk. But I couldn't sleep – it was all so strange – and before long I got up again.

It was evening now, between seven and eight. I wandered along corridors till I found the saloon, and in it my friend of the morning, and another officer who used to visit us in the Fir-Tree Wood. We had dinner together (dinner on a table, off a cloth!); we had a bottle of the bubbly wine; and we drank a solemn toast to the boys we'd left behind us.

I tumbled back to bed, at the close of our very brief meal, too tired and too sore to sleep. I never closed an eye. I felt the screw turn and the great boat throb, and knew that we were steaming away from Lemnos. So in the dark and the silence we crept back over the Aegean, away from the place we had come to six weeks before – a glorious army of young exultant men, strong and unafraid then; now a boatload of broken men, old and very tired.

I lay late the next day. I felt indescribably ill, and I seemed to be losing my memory. In the afternoon I struggled up to have a look round. I could walk with more and more difficulty; but I got hold of a stick and hobbled about the deck. I can never forget that sight. It out-trenched the trenches. It was crueller than the firing-line. Men were lying on stretchers all over the deck, just as they had been picked up after getting first-aid. They were caked with mud, and with dirt that was worse than mud, and with blood. They had the growth of weeks on their sunken faces. Some were dying, and knew it. All were badly hurt, many maimed for life. But every one of them was cheerful.

It was appalling tragedy. The great liner, beautifully appointed, was ploughing its way through a calm sea in bright sunshine, and with just a faint breeze to temper the heat. It was a fit boat for a queen's holiday. The scenery – ill as I was – thrilled me, and I was born and bred in the beauty of Scotland. It was a boat and a day and a scene for song and laughter, and high good spirits and friendliness. There was so much here to enjoy; but instead of the passengers at ease that she and the day and the place catered and called for, the boat lay low under a weight of bleeding, weltering men, over a thousand of them, humanity maimed and mutilated! They had been in the full flower of strength and of manhood but yesterday. And in normal times each would have been making or doing something useful in some peaceful vocation, in some peaceful home-place. Now they lay, pallid and bleeding, on the deck of a misery-packed steamer, going to Alexandria to die, or to have a dangling leg cut off, an aching wound probed and tortured, to be sick and strangled and intolerably thirsty from anaesthetics, to be patched up, if possible, and come back to the hell of battle, the purgatory of the trench.

Yet, with it all, I don't believe that there was even one who regretted that he had come out to do his bit, or who ever had regretted, or ever would regret.

I have seen many a man die. Death and I are 'auld acquaintance' now. Every soldier of ours that I watched set off on the long journey was no coward, but crossed over calmly, with a smile on his white lips and a cheery *au revoir* in his glazing eyes. I remember a dying man saying, I'm going West, sir. I hope the wife and bairns at home will be looked after.' These were the last words he spoke – a rough, uncultured man, maybe; but he had loved his native country, and at the last his thought was all of some small home in a village in Scotland, where a woman fighting bravely to keep that home was together till her husband came back to her. God grant that his last wish may be fulfilled! War is a damnable tragedy. And that its bitterest battles are fought, and lost or won, at the front, no man can say.

Chapter 20

In Hospital

The doctors and the orderlies worked supremely; and that boat was as full of kindness as it was of wounds and woe.

Personally, instead of getting better, I seemed steadily to be getting worse, and the only comfort I got from the M.O. was that I'd be worse yet before I was any better.

We were four days at sea, and then, on just such another morning as we had first seen the lovely, laughing place, we steamed again into Alexandria. The gem city of Egypt had not changed since we left her, leaping expectant towards our fray; but we! —

Most of the officer cases had to go on to Cairo, and I was booked for there. For some reason or other, some sick man's fancy that I cannot recall, I wished to stay in Alexandria, and I managed to work it – how I do not remember either. There's a deal of haze in my mind still about those days.

In the afternoon I was taken off in an ambulance to No. 19 General Hospital. Before the war it had belonged to a German sisterhood!

In the entrance-hall a nurse had a look at the tab on my coat, the tab the doctor had pinned there in Gallipoli. I had never even tried to see what it said, or whether it was in English or Red Cross hieroglyphics. But the nurse understood it, and bundled me off to a ward, and handed me over to another nurse, who ushered me into a cubicle where there already was another officer who seemed to be as silly as I was.

A glass of hot milk, and off I went to bed. But I could not even doze. My cubicle-mate thrashed about and muttered to himself, and I could do nothing but lie very still and wonder what we were doing in Gallipoli. In a very keen and intimate sense I was in the peninsula still. All the time I was in the hospital, every day of my voyage home, and for weeks after that, my spirit seemed to fret and chafe in the trenches, strive and sweat in the firing-lines that I knew so well. You can carry a no-longer-fit soldier's body out of the firing-line, but not his soul; his spirit stays with his unit until the expedition is over.

A doctor came along the next day, and had a look at me, with the result that the following morning I was established on a veranda outside the ward. But still I could not sleep – and, oh! I wanted it so: sleep – and I seemed, too, to be losing the power of speech, and more and more my memory. I tried to remember; it was about the only effort I made, or cared to make. I was anxious not to forget. But I had less than no wish to speak! And I hated having anyone to speak to me.

Hour after hour I lay fretting and striving to recall each item of my Gallipoli weeks, and often failing miserably. But later, with returning health and strength, the memory of those livid weeks came slowly back, until it was as vivid as if it had been clearly printed in large black type on very white paper. And now it seems to me that Gallipoli was but yesterday. And often the street I'm on, in Edinburgh, in London, or in Paris, seems less real to me than the broken goat-paths of Gallipoli.

But even a war-shocked brain cannot resist sleep for ever, and go on living. After a day or two I began to snatch scraps of slumber and oblivion. And, Heaven be praised! I had no dreams. Such sleep as I got I got at night; but no matter how much or how little it was, at half-past two I woke, with an invincible regularity that would have made the fame and fortune of any alarm-clock. I could not read much; it started my head throbbing like the pulsing tom-tom battle-cry of the Turks. The only thing I could do from half-past two in the morning till long after dark at night was to lie still and wait, and gaze at a prison, cheerfully (for us) situated just across the street. That was not particularly interesting, but it was my only form of amusement. I used to lie and watch lazily for the changing of the prison guard. That happened twice daily, at six and at six. The guard was composed of men of the Egyptian Army. All their proceedings were like a bit of Gilbert and Sullivan. Mounting the guard was their masterpiece. I never knew what they'd do next. My sole amusement wasn't half-monotonous. The commanders were of corporal's rank. The old guard would be drawn up, ready to receive the new guard. When the new guard arrived, the corporal in charge would at once shake hands with the corporal of the old guard and, as often as not, then shake hands with one of the rank and file – presumably an old pal. The commanders carried swords; and once I saw one of them strike one of the rank and file across the legs with the flat of his sword, whether in fun, in censure, or in love, I could not determine.

After I had been in hospital four days, I was told that I was to be 'boarded', and that probably I would be 'for England' – the board would decide. For England! I closed my eyes, and set my lips as firmly as I could. England! With Scotland close at hand! Home! I lay very still on my bed, and I could feel the perspiration well up and ooze out of every pore. And I felt my heart flutter against my ribs, as I had never yet felt it in battle.

The sister had told me that I was very ill, but I had never once thought that they might send me home. But they did. I had a few days *and nights* of hideous suspense; doctors to pummel and punch me; a board to sit on me – hard; delays, orders and counter-orders – but at last I went.

While on the peninsula I had thought several times that it must soon be my turn to be hit, and I sensed my final break-down coming; but I had never for an instant thought that I might he killed. I *knew* that I should not be killed. So sure was I of this that, had I been killed, it would have taken a great deal to make me believe it. I have no doubt that there are premonitions that are sure sign-posts on our road of life. All my life I had been sceptical of every claim that even bordered on mysticism – but not now. The Dardanelles convinced me. I know what I know. I saw what I saw. Whether the subtle charm of the East lends itself to psychic revelation as the West never can, I do not know. But I know that there is a veil that is occasionally lifted – and woe is his who endeavours to pierce it to further his own ends.

I had known that I should leave the Dardanelles alive. But I had never thought that I might leave Gallipoli before my battalion did, and perhaps I need not add that that was the last thing I'd have wished. As for going home before my men did, even here, on my back in a hospital cot, it had not crossed my mind at first. But now it was all my thought. It obsessed me. 'I have recommended you for home', the doctor said to me the day before I was 'boarded', and the words are seared into my memory, branded there for ever.

Chapter 21

Going Home

The news – that I was indeed going – made a man of me again. It put bones into my legs; it flushed my veins with red blood. I got up and dressed. I couldn't have run a race, but a stick and I did quite a creditable hobble around that old hospice that had once belonged to a German sisterhood, and that now decidedly did not. I found old friends; I made new ones.

It was a most up-to-date establishment, this ex-German hospital. The operating-theatre was sumptuous – marble-lined, glass, silver, everything perfect. One poor Irish wag, who went into it with two legs and came out with one, looked into it a month afterwards and began to warble, 'I dreamt that I dwelt in marble halls.' The whole place did the Germans great credit. It shone with their thoroughness.

On peeping into one of the cubicles I noticed a poor fellow with both legs and both arms swung in supports from the ceiling. He was absolutely helpless, of course. But two charming V.A.D.s were giving him tea, and making much of him, and he seemed as happy as a well-fed baby. He was an Australian, and he had forty-eight wounds. Not badly played, for a single day's engagement! However, he was getting on famously, and said he'd 'be back soon'. He was chatting and joking and chuckling while he took his tea, and as I hobbled down the corridor I heard a ringing shout of laughter – his.

Again I was on board in the harbour of Alexandria. It was a glorious day. From four till after six I lay on deck and watched the old city of which I had once dreamed so much. And again I was thinking of it but little now. Nor were my thoughts of home. My thoughts were in the trenches of Gallipoli.

We steamed away at seven.

It was an uneventful voyage, and none the worse for that, we thought. 'Rest and routine' describes our life aboard. And my routine consisted chiefly of bed. Almost every one of us grew better rapidly. There is no other panacea half so sure, half so quick, as a sea-voyage is, if it's a smooth one. Ours hadn't a ripple.

Two of our battalion officers were on board – Lieutenants Geddes and Sutherland. We clung together rather pathetically. The subaltern who had been shot through the head had the swinging-cot next to mine. I had seen him in our Alexandrian hospital. I fancy his recovery will go down the medical ages as a miracle. The doctors never tired of watching him, in Egypt or at sea. I was particularly glad that he was going back with me, for I had promised his wife that I would bring him safe home to her. Well, I was bringing him back, and not so much the worse for that hole some Turk had made in his head.

We lay off Malta for a day, and I wheedled a few hours' leave out of the doctor, and drove up to the town. I dismissed my *gharri*, and took a quiet saunter along the Rue de Valetta. But I felt rather sad, recalling the merry party we'd been here on our way out. Most of my companions then I'd never see again.

A figure coming toward me, one arm in a sling, looked familiar. And it was, for it turned out to be the general of my brigade. He had been wounded, so he told me, on the day of my collapse – the 4th of June. He had been at Malta ever since, but now he was going home in our boat.

We sailed again that night.

Prowling about (my inveterate habit always reasserts itself) in the afternoon, I found my old orderly, the chap who, after living a charmed life in the thickest of the danger for weeks, had at last been shot while sitting resting at my dug-out. I was especially glad to find him, for until now I had been unable to learn where he was or how he had fared.

We were gradually drawing towards home.

Our last night out every one in the officers' ward was able to be up – not very martial-looking, some of us, I fear, but getting well – and going home!

We landed the next day, and Lieutenant Sutherland and I went up to London.

Do you care to know what we thought, what we felt, with the Old Country before our hungry sight, the old sod under our war-sick feet? You must try your hand at guessing, then. I've not a word to tell it in. Every blade of English grass looked a jewel. The country – we ate it with our eyes. And the blue above the green was heaven indeed.

It was afternoon when we reached town, and made for a hotel. We had tea in the lounge! Oh, that wonderful tea! I suspect the maid that brought it to us thought we were both mad, and I believe we were – for a time.

The next day we left for Scotland and home.

Epilogue

For nine months in Gallipoli we put up a fight such as the world had never seen before. Besides bearing the brunt of the enemy's instruments of destruction, we were well-nigh destroyed by a plague of flies, and at the last we were all but frozen out. The rain came, and washed the splendid remnants of the 29th Division from their trenches, and floated off their food and their few belongings like corks on Niagara Rapids. Dysentery almost decimated us.

But none of this was why we left. We left because we wished to leave. Our landing was a triumph; our going was a triumph. The battered peninsula was free once more to lick its wounds of war – the natives to come out of hiding – the currant and the olive to leaf and fruit, if any bush or tree remained not blasted by the guns.

The scene of battle was staged near that of the Trojans. In reading the histories and the epics of long ago one used to marvel at ancient deeds of valour and medieval heroism. We can never so marvel again. They have been surpassed by shopkeepers from Antrim, Dundee, and London; by navvies and farmhands and miners from Kent, Clare, Argyll, and Glamorgan; by men and boys from every nook and corner of our Empire – Australasia, Canada, Africa, India, a thousand islands, that used to mean to us geography and the map: they mean brotherhood now! Think of the picture they made in this wild, picturesque place!

The trend of the people in 1914 made you fear that the brave old days, the loyal days, were gone for ever. Their pockets and their dinners seemed the only concern of our pampered proletariat. But they wronged themselves. At core they were sounder than their self-centred attitude. They grumbled as the door of the fiery furnace opened, but they did not baulk at it. They passed in, and it has tried and proved them. And this carnage of human life has proved that the old British breed is grit through and through. It was dormant in some, but not dead, not enfeebled, not tainted. A nation of shopkeepers! Let us leave it at that; let us make it our boast – shopkeepers that have organised and extemporised the greatest departmental store in the world – with unlimited credit. And it isn't being run this time for the benefit of foreigners, dumping their surplus stock. When we have finished with some of them, they'll not have much surplus stock to dump.

And Tommy! Ah, it is not possible to transcribe to paper that wonderful person called Thomas Atkins. The officers who have fought beside him, and listened with a sympathetic ear to his various troubles – most of them imagined (for he must have his grouse) – know and love him. When he comes home, may the country he has fought for give him justice, not tosh or coddling. Pitfalls will be many about him, and snares lie thick at his feet. Hold out a strong hand to him, Britain! He has made you. Help him to make himself to a fine manhood and a worthy citizenship in the greatest Empire of earth or of time, made supreme in her greatness by the force of her foes and the loyal might of her sons.

THE END